HISPANIC AMERICANS
in the
CIVIL WAR

HISPANIC AMERICANS
in the
CIVIL WAR

A.J. SCHENKMAN

THE
History
PRESS

Published by The History Press
An imprint of Arcadia Publishing
Charleston, SC
www.historypress.com

First published 2025

Manufactured in the United States

ISBN 9781467155625

Library of Congress Control Number: 2024951967

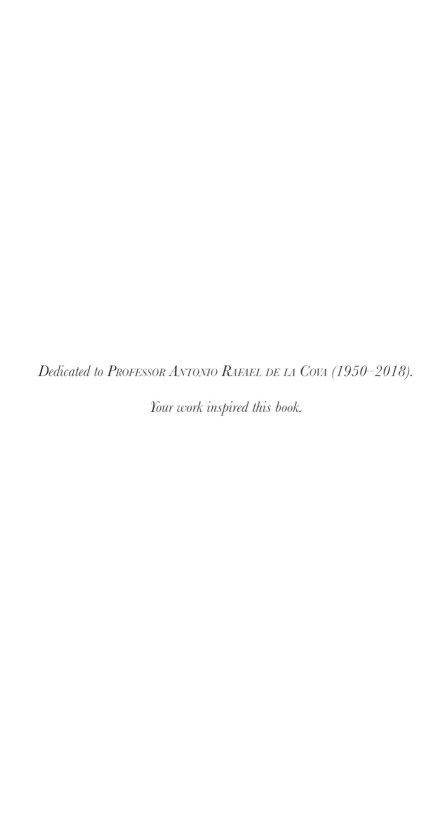

Dedicated to Professor Antonio Rafael de la Cova (1950–2018).

Your work inspired this book.

Contents

PREFACE

I have always held a passion for history. My family would plan trips to museums, Civil War battlefields and presidential libraries as some examples. As a child, I sometimes got my hands on an old penny. I would stare at it, wondering whose hands it passed through. Growing up in Queens, my favorite books were on history, especially local history; I even went as far as volunteering at a Dutch farmstead from the 1600s. Still later, when I was in school in Boston for music—don't ask me why—I spent hours at a time in the old burial grounds, Salem and old churches. I transferred from Boston to New Paltz, where the Hudson Valley and my college courses ignited a full-blown passion. I worked at more historic sites and even started writing for local newspapers. I became involved at local historical societies and libraries. There was so much to explore. It was logical to pursue history by way of teaching. The idea of talking about history all day was inspiring to me.

They say, "Time flies when you are having fun." I have been teaching history for roughly thirty years, and there is still so much to learn. My goal as a writer and teacher has always been to make history more accessible to more people and, most of all, not boring. Since those college days, I found myself being not only a (now former) consulting historian for Historic Huguenot Street but also a municipal historian in New York State. I continue to write, having started off as a writer for newspapers, magazines and, of course, books. My recent book has been a labor of love.

Currently, I am a seventh-grade social studies teacher in New York State. Many of my books have been conceived via simple questions asked by students or mentioned in a reading. In my long career, I have watched the makeup of my classes change. Students have started to probe and ask questions about their heritage within U.S. history. Their questions stimulated my curiosity, resulting in many e-mails, books, research and listening.

My research started with my school textbook, which had very little information pertaining to Hispanics in the Civil War. While looking in my classroom, I stumbled on a National Park Service booklet on Hispanics in this war. This gave me a jumping-off point to discover the scope and context of the subject. After reading and Googling, I had to decide who I would choose to include in my book. After much deliberation, I decided to create a mix of well-known people like Farragut and lesser-known people like Thomas Hernandez. It was easier to write about well-known individuals because there was so much more information. Many hours were spent in libraries and archives, communicating with experts in the field and finally searching many newspapers for many of these lesser-known individuals.

This book is a lesson in history that, sadly, many Americans do not know. I did not know before this book that there was a vibrant Puerto Rican community in both Connecticut and New York before the Civil War. I also did not know that Mexico ended slavery in 1829. This was more than three decades before the Emancipation Proclamation and the Thirteenth Amendment. Mexico's commitment to end slavery was so strong that it even created a route for those escaping from enslavement to make their way to Mexico and freedom. This means that an Underground Railroad ran both North and South. This topic was both fascinating and engaging.

First and foremost, this is a book about people. It is less about the complex battles that, in some cases, they participated in or played a role in during their lifetime. I hope the reader walks away with a sense of the individuals contained within this book. I hope you will agree and enjoy the book.

ACKNOWLEDGEMENTS

To the following people and organizations, and to the many more I might have accidently forgotten, thank you so much. I could not have done it without you:

PATRICIA TANNER, ST. AUGUSTINE Genealogical Society; Katy Lockard, director, Archives and Records Catholic Diocese of St. Augustine; Terri Sowards, St. Ambrose Catholic Church; Father Steven Zehler; Charles Tingley, senior research librarian, St. Augustine Historical Society; Holly Baker, archivist, Library of Florida History; Chelsea Joslin, State Archives Florida; Molly Copeland, manuscript archivist; Kyle A. Williams; Libbie Werlau; Special Collections University of Tennessee at Chattanooga; Monica Toth, archivist, State Archives of Florida; Caroline Galt, University of North Carolina–Chapel Hill graduate assistant; Jacob Rader Marcus; Center of the American Jewish Archives; Patricia Clark, New Haven County Clerk's Office; Ruth E. Lloyd Information Center for Genealogy and Local History; Prince William Public Libraries; Historical Society of Pennsylvania; David Kahn, archivist, Central High School; Juan A. Villanueva, Cuban Heritage Collection and Spanish Language Collection University of Florida Miami; Brad Coker; Robert Redd; Georgia Archives; Georgia Historical Society; New York State Library; Naval History and Heritage Command; U.S. Army Heritage and Education Center; Virginia L. Ellison, South Carolina Historical

Society; North Haven Historical Society; Library of Congress; National Archives and Records Administration; Gopher Records Retrieval; Elisabeth Chappell, education specialist, Coastal Heritage Society; Mike Gorman; Kate Jenkins; John Rodrigue; Ryan Finn; Joyce Faust, the Jewish Museum of New York; University of Tennessee Library Special Collections; Ronald S. Coddington, *Military Images* magazine; Maria Paxi, North Haven Historical Society; Museum of Connecticut History; South Carolina Historical Society; Terry Reimer, director, Research National Museum of Civil War Medicine; Historical Society of Pennsylvania; Mark Bender, Civil War Museum of Philadelphia Museum; Keith Vezeau, military archivist, Massachusetts Archives; Cary Hutto, director, Archives Historical Society of Pennsylvania; Special Collections, University of Tennessee, Knoxville; New York State Military Museum; Erin Beasley, National Portrait Gallery, Washington, D.C.; Peter Maugle; Dr. Matthew T. Pearcy; Dr. John O'Neil, Hispanic Society; my wife; our son; my team members; and my students.

INTRODUCTION

The American Civil War lasted from 1861 to 1865. It was a struggle over the very fabric of the nation. It is well known that it tore apart the nation and pitted families against each other. The Hispanic communities in the United States were no different. In its booklet *Hispanics and the Civil War*, the National Park Service stated succinctly that "thousands of Hispanic civilians lent heart and hands on the home front." Whether this was in some cases working as spies, simply providing supplies or donations or participating directly by enlisting in the armed forces, the reasons for joining were many. It ranged from earning a wage to bounties offered for enlistment or to improve their way of life. Still others looked for the prestige of becoming officers if they were from the upper rungs of society. It is believed that some twenty thousand Hispanics joined the Civil War.

Teaching about the Civil War is seen through the lenses of the North and South, the Union and Confederacy, and the struggle over slavery and states' rights. What is often overlooked are the contributions and experiences of various ethnic groups, including Hispanic Americans. This diverse group includes people of Mexican, Cuban, Puerto Rican, Spanish and Latin American backgrounds. In some cases, these groups played a crucial role in the Civil War. In this book, I will highlight their military contributions to the Civil War on both sides of the conflict.

At the time the American Civil War began in April 1861, Americans of Spanish heritage lived in almost all areas of the country. Some were descendants of Spanish explorers, and still others immigrated to the United States for a better life or were living in areas incorporated into the United States, most notably the Southwest, after the Mexican-American War. Where they lived, in some ways, dictated where they stood on the main issue of the Civil War, which was slavery. Those Hispanics living in the southeastern part of the United States often supported the Confederacy. Another example was those Hispanic Americans who lived in Texas. This state had a significant Tejano population; many of them were large landowners and, hence, in some cases, were tied to the perpetuation of slavery. Those who lived in the New England states mostly supported abolitionism. These, of course, are generalizations. Included in their allegiances were also economic interests and their personal beliefs about slavery, as well as the role of the federal government and the state governments in their lives.

Hispanics served on the homefront in the North and South as well as in the infantry. However, their role in the North and South navies is often overlooked—in fact, the first admiral in U.S. naval history was Hispanic. Also included were men who were awarded the Congressional Medal of Honor. Despite significant contributions to the American Civil War on both sides of the conflict, their roles have often been overshadowed by larger-than-life figures like Lee, Grant and Lincoln. The purpose of this book is to shed some light on the contributions of Hispanics in the Civil War. It is heavier on the biographical end than on the battle end of it. I hope to place the individual within the battle. I included some well-known individuals, such as Admiral Farragut, and lesser-known individuals, like Thomas Hernandez, who was a Southern blockade runner in Georgia. Finally, I wanted to show the diverse contributions of the Hispanic community as a whole.

If Hispanics were from diverse economic backgrounds and different regions of the United States, they also came from different countries. Some individuals came from Mexico, which had declared its independence from Spain in 1821 and later abolished slavery in 1837. Some soldiers and sailors traced their families to Cuba and Puerto Rico, which were still part of Spain, or even from Spain itself. Finally, many families living in Florida came from the Balearic Islands in the Mediterranean Sea. These islands belonged to Spain.

Hispanics were present at many of the most famous battles in the Civil War, both land and sea, including Gettysburg, Fredericksburg and Chancellorsville, as well as epic sea battles such as Mobile Bay. The acting surgeon general for the Confederate army, appointed by the president of the Confederacy, Jefferson Davis, was from Spain. Hispanic Americans served in logistical roles and still others as spies. Hispanic Americans were represented at just about every level of the Civil War.

Part I

The Union

Augusto Rodriguez

I have the honor to request that a "leave of absence" for (48) forty-eight hours may be granted me to go to New Berne, N.C. to procure my clothing.
—Augusto Rodriguez

On April 15, 1861, just three days after the attack on Fort Sumter, President Abraham Lincoln issued a proclamation. In this proclamation, he called for the state militias to supply seventy-five thousand troops to suppress the Southern rebellion. The response was tremendous. General William Tecumseh Sherman's brother, Senator John Sherman, wrote, "The response of the loyal states to the call of Lincoln was perhaps the most remarkable uprising of a great people in the history of mankind." On April 16, Connecticut Governor William A. Buckingham issued a call to the citizens of his state. The volunteers would be required to sign on for three months. Many, probably even Augusto Rodriguez, felt that three months would be all that would be needed. Many felt that the rebellion would be short-lived, with the North quickly defeating the South. In addition to the idea of honor, the pay was also enticing. Sheldon Thorpe, who compiled a history of the 15th Regiment of Connecticut, wrote that the state bounty was fifty dollars upon enlistment, and within a year, an additional thirty dollars would be issued, with a monthly pay of twelve dollars. This was if the war lasted a year. Regarding Augusto, the money promised to him if he enlisted had to be more than what he made at the time as a grocer's clerk.

Augusto Rodriguez resided in an area of Connecticut known as North Haven. It was part of New Haven County in Eastern Connecticut. According to the North Haven Historical Society, farming and industry were the main vocations here in the mid-1800s. Like the rest of New England, the Industrial Revolution took hold in North Haven. One of the biggest employers in the area was David Clinton, who founded the Clintonville Agricultural Works factory. Augusto Rodriguez, a resident of North Haven, decided to volunteer for military service on April 22, 1861. He was mustered into service on May 7, 1861. Rodriguez was placed in the 2nd Connecticut Infantry, Company G, as a private. After serving three months, Rodriguez was mustered out on August 7, 1861.

War fever continued to sweep not only North Haven but also New Haven as a whole. The First Battle of Bull Run (or First Manassas, as the South referred to it) proved to the Union that the war would most likely be a long one. So, on July 2, 1862, President Lincoln called for 300,000 volunteers for three years. Lincoln wrote in his proclamation, "I suggest and recommend that the troops should be chiefly of infantry." He hoped that increasing troops would "bring this unnecessary and injurious war to a speedy and satisfactory conclusion." According to Sheldon Thorpe's history of the 15th Connecticut Infantry, "Connecticut as fixed by a portion was 7145." A few days later, a recruiting station opened in New Haven. According to the regimental history, on July 14, 1862, there was a public call for volunteers. Eventually, there would be "10 offices opened in New Haven, and two in nearby Meridian. Captain Samuel Tolls, of New Haven, would be selected a major."

On July 23, 1862, Rodriguez's name was wrongly recorded as "Augustus Rodereques," yet twenty-four-year-old Augusto was mustered into the 15th Connecticut as a private. He lived, according to the 1860 federal census, on Columbus Avenue. He was paid a sign-on bounty of twenty-five dollars. On July 18, the regiment was to meet at "Oyster Point," named for the oyster industry that was booming at the time on the Long Island Sound. The name given to the 15th and the camp was Lyon, named in honor of Connecticut General Nathaniel Lyon, who was killed in the Battle of Wilson's Creek in August 1861. Dexter R. Wright of Meridian, Connecticut, became the colonel of the 15th. By August 6, 1862, all the companies, A through K, had been assembled. Augusto Rodriguez had signed on for three years of service with Company I, making him the first known Puerto Rican to enlist in the nation's armed forces.

According to his compiled military service, located in the National Archives in Washington, D.C., Rodriguez was born in San Juan, Puerto

Rico, in 1841. Puerto Rico was still part of the Spanish empire and would remain so until 1898, when the United States acquired it after the Spanish-American War. This is why Augusto's place of birth is sometimes recorded as Spain. According to the 1860 federal census, along with the Rodriguez, there were ten families living in North Haven. Sometime during the 1850s, his family immigrated to North Haven, Connecticut. According to his enlistment papers, Augusto Rodriquez stood five-foot-five and had a fair complexion, hazel eyes and brown hair. Although mustered in as a private, Augusto was quickly commissioned as a sergeant in Company I. On August 12, 1862, the 15th Regiment reached full strength.

Rodriguez's first role while in Camp Lyon was guard duty. Sergeant Rodriguez was quite aware of the fundamental problems plaguing the 15th Regiment. Although mustered and in uniform, the 15th still lacked proper arms. In fact, some men had outdated muskets. Eventually, they would be sent proper rifles, but that would come in the future. On August 25, the regiment was mustered into United States service; the same day, the "state colors were formally presented by the ladies of Meridian." Just before leaving New Haven, as printed in the *New Haven Columbia Register*, "August D. Rodriguez and Eliza Hickox" were wed on August 26, 1862. The newlyweds had little time to spend with each other, for the 15th was to leave New Haven in two days. Sheldon Thorpe, also a sergeant in the 15th, wrote that the regiment was paid just prior to leaving New Haven.

The 15th or Lyon Regiment prepared to depart New Haven on August 28. Local newspapers recorded that it was a stormy morning, but by the time they were ready to board the train, the sun was shining—a good omen to the soldiers but also probably more comfortable. Augusto and the 15th were bound for New York City, which they reached early in the evening, "disembarking at 42nd Street." From this point, the regiment marched "down 4th Avenue and Broadway to the Battery," named for the artillery batteries that were built in the late seventeenth century to protect the settlement in its early years. Sergeant Rodriguez would have been greeted by large crowds of people lining both sides of Broadway. Thorpe recorded that Sergeant Rodriguez and Company I were singing "Glory, Hallelujah" in a heavy thunderstorm that did not dampen their spirits. This song, believed to be written by Julia Ward Howe, a prominent abolitionist, is also known as "The Battle Hymn of the Republic." When the 15th arrived at the Battery, the regiment then departed for South Amboy, New Jersey, and then by rail to Camden, New Jersey; by early Friday morning on August 29, 1862, they were all in Philadelphia. While there, Thorpe remembered a large breakfast being served to the troops by local organizations.

They arrived in Baltimore on the evening of August 29. Baltimore was sometimes a hostile city to Union troops, although it would remain loyal to the Union. The men were only allowed to leave the train to sleep in the depot. When they awoke, the last leg of their journey would take them to the nation's capital. When they arrived, they were served dinner and then marched down Pennsylvania Avenue to Arlington Heights, with its commanding view of Washington, D.C. They had arrived in the capital on August 30, 1862, at noon, according to Thorpe.

Arlington belonged to Robert E. Lee and his wife, Mary Custis, the daughter of General George Washington's grandson George Washington Parke Custis. If Virginia left the Union, Lee maintained that he, too, would join the Confederacy. The mansion overlooked Washington, D.C., and would need to be taken by federal troops, which is what happened. According to Arlington National Cemetery, "The U.S. Army seized Arlington Estate on the morning of May 24, 1861, to defend Washington, D.C. from the property's heights, rifled artillery could range every federal building in the nation's capital." Augusto and the 15th were tasked with guarding the Long Bridge.

According to the Department of Transportation for Washington, D.C., "In 1808, by an Act of Congress signed into law by President Thomas Jefferson, the 'Long Bridge' was constructed as a toll crossing of the Potomac River….Only foot, horse, and stagecoach traffic used the structure until the mid-1850s." While Rodriguez was guarding the bridge, a rail was added to the bridge. It was vital to protect the bridge because it had direct access to Washington, D.C.

When he arrived on August 30, Rodriguez and the rest of the 15th could hear the second Battle of Bull Run in the distance, which was fought August 28–30, 1862. It was roughly twenty-five miles away from their location; unfortunately for Rodriguez and the rest of the troops, they had marched at such a quick pace that they preceded the arrival of their tents as well as their rations. It is important to note that they still did not have proper rifles, so they were to sit out the battle. They were also forced to sleep on the ground without supper while they waited for their supply train to catch up to them. Deprivation would figure into Rodriguez's later disability when he applied for a pension after the war.

The next day, August 31, 1862, adequate rifles finally arrived. They were Whitney rifles, according to Thorpe, who remembered it as

September 1; the regiment appreciated them because they were lighter than the more common Springfield. In addition, the Whitney rifle was from New Haven, where the Whitney Armory stood on the banks of the Mill River. According to Colonel George M. White, captain of Company E, 15th Connecticut Volunteers:

> Orders were received on September 5th for the regiment to join the Union forces hurrying into Maryland to repel the invasion of Lee's army, but they were at once countermanded, and during that critical period the Fifteenth continued guarding Long Bridge, a part of the time encamped near the unfinished Washington monument, but most of the time at "Camp Chase," on Arlington Heights. Here it remained until November, the night duty in the malarial atmosphere and fogs of the Potomac flats working serious harm to the health of the men.

Later that month, "on September 27, the 15th was made part of the General Kanes brigade" and put under "marching orders with 10 days rations, and 100 rounds of ammunition per man." The orders were then countermanded. The next day, they were ordered to remain in Camp Chase on Arlington Heights. Recently, the regiment had been vaccinated and was considered unfit to march; also, a large percentage of the 15th was currently sick. Thorpe believed, like Colonel White, that it was due to the proximity to the marshes around the nation's capital. While not sick, he wrote, "The regiment was first initiated into the never to be forgotten luxury of 'scratching itself to sleep.'"—no doubt because of fleas. There is no indication from his service record that Augusto was sick. On October 2, the regiment was brought under the 12th New Hampshire, 17th New York and 157th Pennsylvania, to be called the 1st Provisional Brigade for the Defense of Washington.

The 15th was aching for battle, and that time would come soon. Colonel White remembered that during the month of November, the regiment was in camp at what was called the Fairfax Seminary, located in Virginia. The men were guarding an extended picket line, "attending numerous parades and reviews, and suffering fearfully from malaria contracted while on duty at Long Bridge." Thanksgiving was celebrated on November 27, 1862, and would be remembered by all for lots of boxes and packages that arrived from New Haven. These packages made the holiday special for the men, who were so far away from home, many for the first time in their lives.

Early in December 1862, the 15th received orders to march down the Maryland side of the Potomac. They would reach the Aquia Creek in Virginia and eventually cross the creek, camping in "eight inches of snow." They were forced to sleep without tents or even the ability to cook rations. The cold weather and having to sleep on the ground, without adequate protection, started to take their toll on the health of Augusto Rodriguez.

On December 10, 1862, the 15th became part of the "Connecticut Brigade," camping at Falmouth, Virginia, opposite Fredericksburg. Augusto recorded, almost ten years later, that the exposure of a march in winter, from the camp near "Fairfax seminary to Falmouth via Acquia Creek…induced an attack of inflammatory rheumatism." This was his first attack recorded. Although he was in tremendous pain, his compiled military service record did not show him being absent from duty, even while Union troops were massing for an attack on Fredericksburg, Virginia.

Again, according to Colonel White's report, the "attack on Fredericksburg began with heavy artillery on December 11th." The 15th was switched to "Harland's Brigade." This was made up of the 8th, 11th, 15th, 16th and 21st Connecticut Regiments. They would make up the 3rd Brigade, 1st Division, and 9th Army Corps. This was in an attempt to silence the sharpshooters harassing Union troops. The 15th had crossed the Rappahannock River by late morning on December 12, into Fredericksburg and created a camp in the streets of the city. The men had to contend with shells from both armies flying overhead. A fog, combined with the smoke from burning houses, created a thick soup that just hung over the city, making it very difficult to see or breathe. Sergeant Thorpe wrote, "About 3 o'clock the fog lifted, uncovering the Confederate lines on Marye's Heights." As soon as the Confederates on the heights saw that the Union troops were in range, they opened fire on them.

Early the next morning, after some quick rations, the attack commenced. Sergeant Rodriguez and the rest of the 15th were held in reserve for the entire day until early evening. When the 15th was led into the assault, Sergeant Rodriguez guided Company I in an attack on Marye's Heights. Thorpe, who was in the fray, remembered that there was a swift advance through a field, "then over a stream, and across a meadow to the cover of a slight rise of ground afforded." Here the line halted and dressed; a few were wounded, but ten seconds later, "such a storm of lead and iron broke over the swamp just crossed as would have decimated any force there."

On December 14, 1862, the 15th made its way back to the city to reform for another anticipated attack against the Confederates. However, the attack never materialized; the Army of the Potomac began its retreat, while the 15th covered the retreat at the rear. It would be one of the very last regiments to leave the city and cross the Rappahannock River. From Christmas 1862 to January 6, 1863, the 15th busied itself readying its winter quarters near Fredericksburg.

General Burnside did not want to admit defeat. He looked for an opportunity to reverse his fortunes at Fredericksburg. He ordered the Army of the Potomac to move on January 20, 1863. According to the National Park Service, Burnside hoped to cross "the Rappahannock River at Banks' Ford placing his army directly in Lee's rear." While this was happening, other troops would create a decoy at the "same river crossings across from Fredericksburg the Army of the Potomac had used one month before." However, the winter weather had transitioned to warmer weather, turning the solid ground into mud. It was followed by heavy rain. The mud became so deep and thick in some places that it bogged down the Union forces. It would become known as the "Mud March." Burnside's hopes were dashed, as his element of surprise was discovered by Lee and his Army of Northern Virginia. Many men, maybe even an ailing Rodriguez, breathed a sigh of relief, as it probably would have ended with many men dying. Once again, the 15th returned to winter quarters.

After Fredericksburg, the 15th was occupied by camp duties and the ordinary alarms until February 6, 1863. By February 8, 1863, they had arrived in Newport News, Virginia. The first thing Rodriguez and others would have noticed was the new barracks, which were spacious and warm. They remained here for about a month. Rodriguez wrote after the war that even "with the severity of the attacks," while in the army "he was never in any hospital under treatment; that when I was attacked with the rheumatism my regiment was on the march." He went on to say that there were no hospitals anyway. His comrades frequently took care of him until he was better.

After Newport News, the 15th left its comfortable barracks for Norfolk, Virginia. From here it marched to Suffolk, Virginia, "where it went into camp west of the town." On March 14, 1863, the camp was located near the Nansemond River. A spring storm, according to Thorpe, added to the misery of the march. It left almost one foot of snow on the ground. White wrote that their camp was commanded by General Peck. "He soon had all the troops shoveling dirt and making gabions in defense of a place which seemed destitute of strategical importance." White continued, noting that by April 10, the reason for it had become apparent.

Confederate General James Longstreet laid siege to the Union troops in what would be called the Siege of Suffolk. This lasted from April 15 to May 4, 1863. According to the adjutant general's report, from the raising of the siege until June 20, the regiment was very pleasantly quartered in various camps in or near Suffolk. On the latter date, it took the railroad for Portsmouth and soon after arrived there to join the raid up the Peninsula organized by General John Adams Dix.

The Peninsula Raid was an attempt to draw Lee from Pennsylvania by threatening the Confederate capital of Richmond. "On July 4th, the Union forces were within twelve miles of Richmond, but Lee was already fleeing from Gettysburg, and it was too late to take Richmond by surprise," again according to the report. This long, arduous march left the 15th in what has been described as a dilapidated state. It had marched some 120 miles in the southern summer heat. Eventually, the men marched back to Portsmouth and remained there until January 1864. Their next journey would be by steamer to Morehead, North Carolina, where they arrived on January 23, 1864. Augusto Rodriquez penned a resignation from the 15th, Company I, on April 13, 1864, in order to accept his new commission as a second lieutenant. By order of General John J. Peck, he would remain in the same regiment and company.

By April 19, 1864, the 15th was in Little Washington, North Carolina. Confederate General Robert F. Hoke had captured almost three thousand Union soldiers, including the 16th Connecticut Infantry. He threatened Little Washington with an attack. The attack never came, and Union General Edward Harland ordered all forts to be dismantled and buildings burned while retreating to Newbern. The 15th remained at Newbern on provost duty. This would be the role of military police in today's army. They continued in this role until December 9, 1864.

In early December 1864, Rodriguez was heading with the 15th to Kinston, North Carolina. Its objective was to surprise Kinston by crossing the Neuse River and destroying the Rebel supplies in order to occupy the attention of the Confederates. The hope was that while they were distracted, it would allow General Ulysses S. Grant to "extend his lines in the direction of Weldon, North Carolina." Unfortunately, the river was so swollen from the rain that the troops could not get across it. They returned to Newbern. Confederate reinforcements started to arrive, making an attack on Newbern unlikely.

The next battle that would require the 15th, according to historian Daniel W. Barefoot, was the Battle of Wyse Fork, also known as the Battle of Southwest Creek. It took place March 8–10, 1865. Barefoot wrote that it was "a fierce engagement between Union and Confederate forces near Kinston, North Carolina." Major General William T. Sherman entered North Carolina early in March 1865, heading for Goldsboro. According to Barefoot, "Three divisions under Major General Jacob D. Cox had left any Newbern to join forces with Sherman."

General Joseph E. Johnston now had to prevent the rendezvous of Sherman with Cox. Confederate General Braxton Bragg was tasked with that responsibility. This occurred east of Kinston at Southwest Creek. General Robert F. Hoke and Colonel Daniel Harvey Hill were in command. On March 8, the Confederates flanked the Union soldiers, including the 15th. Thorpe wrote that the attack was so rapid that the Union and the 15th were "swept away." They were forced to fall back. The 15th desperately tried to regroup but fell back again. Eventually, Rodriguez and most of the 15th ran right into the Rebels and were forced to surrender. Thorpe wrote, "The state colors were with Company C, in the left wing." They had to be given up. The U.S. flag was never given up—it was with the right wing.

Once captured, Thorpe noted, the 15th was stripped of anything of value or use to the Rebel soldiers. The wounded were taken to a field hospital. Able-bodied soldiers were marched across the creek and up to Kinston. Eventually, Rodriguez was placed in Libby Prison in Richmond, Virginia. Rodriguez was captured at Southwest Creek on March 8, 1865.

Rodriguez arrived at Libby Prison on March 17, 1865. Thorpe wrote that all were utterly exhausted: "They dropped where they halted." Rodriguez could not have known how short a time he would be held captive because the war was rapidly coming to an end. According to a memorandum from prisoners of war records, Augusto was paroled on March 26 under the name Rodrick. Although he was paroled in March and sent to a parole camp in Maryland, the date is not recorded. It was not until April 30, 1865, that he was formally exchanged and ordered back to his regiment. In addition, back pay was granted to him.

Shortly after his release, Second Lieutenant Rodriguez requested a leave of thirty days to go back to Connecticut "to exercise the elective franchise"—he wanted to vote in an election. This leave was granted from March 27 to April 6, 1865. He was listed in a War Department memo of March 31, 1865, and signed by Assistant Adjutant General Edward D. Townsend as "Second Lieutenant Augustus Rodrick." When researching his life, the different ways in which his name is incorrectly spelled make it very difficult to find him.

The Civil War ended on April 9, 1865. Augusto was still obligated to return to his company and regiment, only to request leave again. In a letter he penned to his captain, he asked for a forty-eight-hour pass to Newbern, North Carolina, to "retrieve my clothing." He reported back for duty on May 15, 1865. Second Lieutenant Augusto Rodriguez was finally discharged from the 15th Connecticut on June 27, 1865. He was officially mustered out of service in New Haven on July 12, 1865.

Once Rodriguez returned to New Haven, he resumed his job as a grocer's clerk, where he worked prior to the war. According to the *Benham New Haven Directory* for 1866, Augusto worked at 247 State Street, and his home was on 142 George Street, where he lived with Eliza, his wife, and a newborn daughter, Clara A. Throughout the 1860s, he remained employed as a clerk but moved to different residences, including 6 Artisan Street. The last year he was a grocery clerk was recorded in the federal census for 1870. However, his residence continued to be listed as 6 Artisan Street. In the following two years, 1871 and 1872, Augustus disappeared from the local business directories.

As far as we know, Augusto Rodriguez first applied for a pension in 1873. The reason he gave, confirmed by a surgeon's certificate, was inflammatory rheumatism. Augusto asserted that this affliction was acquired in the army during his time in Fredericksburg. He asserted, under oath, that it disabled him. Augusto wrote that his address in 1873 was presently 289 Grand Street. A reason for not being mentioned in the business directory was due to "repeated attacks of the rheumatism" contracted in the army such that he had been "obliged to discontinue work" for the last five months and had been totally disabled for the previous nine months. Effectively, because of his disability, Augusto was unable "to earn anything during said times." He had other attacks prior to requesting a pension that rendered him unable to work, including in October 1867. According to a letter written by his doctor on September 4, 1872, to the Superior Court of New Haven County, the attacks occurred mainly in his "hands and feet." In addition to the inflammatory rheumatism, the doctor noted that he also developed "valvular of the heart." The Bureau of Pensions granted him a pension of two dollars per month.

We do not know if he left his job as a clerk or was fired because of the frequency and duration of the attacks. According to the 1874 *Benham Directory for New Haven County*, Augusto worked for or owned a cigar store at 122 Union Street. Two years later, in 1876, his occupation was listed as bartender, and he lived at 344 State Street. As the rheumatism grew worse, he earned less and less money. In 1879, Augusto applied for an increase in his pension. In a letter to the Superior Court for New Haven County on October 16, 1879, Dr. Bissell wrote regarding his patient Augusto that the "pensioner has the appearance of being broken down in constitution." He also noted in his report that Augusto had limited mobility. The reason, in his opinion, was "swelling of the ankle, joints, and hands." Additionally, he was weakened because of a "bilious murmur and hypertrophy of the heart." In his opinion, Rodriquez was completely disabled. Augusto was just thirty-eight years old. He still managed to be employed. The same year, 1879, according to Price, Lee and Company's *New Haven Directory*, he was a "saloon keeper" living at 65 Union Street. It would be his last year of life.

His certificate of death, recording his full name as Gustave Rodriguez, stated that he died on March 22, 1880, at his home. It listed his home as 50 Union Street, New Haven, Connecticut. His home was actually next door at 48 Union Street. Why he was next door is not noted. His last recorded occupation was noted as saloon keeper. The cause of death was listed as a disease of the heart. What is interesting is that he was listed on his death certificate as divorced. There is no existing record of him divorcing his wife. He was interred at the Evergreen Cemetery in the Firefighter Pantheon. The cemetery is located in New Haven County. He was a volunteer firefighter, although it's not entirely clear how since he was so disabled from the time he came back from the Civil War until his death.

Philip Bazaar

*Please send my bounty by Adam's Express to Norfolk, Va.…
I am now in the need of it.*

—*Philip Bazaar*

The entry into the Congressional Medal of Honor file for June 22, 1865, was simple. It recorded that "Philip Bazaar ordinary seamen," with four other men—John Griffiths, Edward Swatton, John Swanson and George Province—were all aboard the USS *Santiago de Cuba*. According to General Order no. 59, the men were part of "a boat's crew detailed for General Terry. They are represented to have been the only men who entered Fort Fisher in the assault from the Fleet, January 15, 1865."

Ordinary Seaman (OS) Bazaar was the second Hispanic U.S. Navy sailor to win the Congressional Medal of Honor. According to the Congressional Medal of Honor Society, the medal is "the United States' highest award for military valor in action. And while over 150 years have passed since its inception, the meaning behind the Medal has never been tarnished. Etched within are the very values that each Recipient displayed in the moments that mattered—bravery, courage, sacrifice, integrity. A deep love of country and a desire to always do what is right." The first Hispanic person to win the Congressional Medal of Honor was John Ortega on December 31, 1864. He was a seaman aboard the USS *Saratoga*. His citation reads that Ortega conducted himself "gallantly"

Battle of Fort Fisher. *Naval History and Heritage Command.*

during several raids in South Carolina while part of the South Atlantic Blockading Squadron. He was promoted to master's mate in June 1865. How did Philip Bazaar, an immigrant from Chile, become part of the American Civil War, let alone the second Hispanic in naval history to win this prestigious award?

Philip Bazaar was born on February 18, 1845, according to the 12th U.S. Census, taken in 1900. The same document states that he was born in Valparaiso, Chile, in the western part of that country, on the Pacific Ocean. Philip immigrated with his family to the United States around 1848. His family eventually settled in Harwich, Massachusetts, which is located on Cape Cod. Harwich was known in the nineteenth century for cranberries and was also a whaling port. Little is known about his family or where they lived in Harwich. The local historical society had no records of the family's time spent in Harwich. One of our best documents is the federal census. We can extrapolate that Philip did attend school because he was able to read and write in English. We also have his naturalization papers, which demonstrate that he became a naturalized citizen by 1863 during the Civil War. Although some historians assert that he was born in the 1830s, the federal census, as well as his later military enlistment record, clearly states that he was eighteen in 1864. It is not known for sure why he enlisted in the Union navy. It could have been his belief that slavery was wrong or loyalty to the Union. It also might have been the three-year sign-on bounty. Later, when stationed in Norfolk, Virginia, in 1865, he wrote a letter home, asking to be sent the bounty money owed to him because he needed it for expenses.

Bazaar did not enlist in Harwich but rather in New Bedford, Massachusetts, which would have been roughly forty miles away. He enlisted on May 18, 1864. In his paperwork, it does not mention any sea experience. However, he was listed as an ordinary seaman, meaning that he probably had previous experience or served at least two years in the navy. His enlistment records in the Massachusetts State Archives have his name recorded as "Philip Bazan," which, of course hampers research into his life. At the time Philip enlisted, the doctor described him as having black hair, black eyes and a dark complexion and being about five-foot-six. Additionally, he had a mole on his left cheek and an "anchor" on his right leg. One can assume that this was a tattoo, further bolstering the idea that he had prior experience on the sea.

Once he was mustered into the U.S. Navy, his first assignment was on the USS *Ohio*. Later, he was transferred to the USS *Santiago de Cuba*, which was under the command of Admiral David D. Porter. The *Santiago*, according to the U.S. Navy, was "a side-wheel steamship acquired by the Union Navy during the first year of the American Civil War." As a gunboat, it had twenty-pound rifled guns as well as thirty-two-pound cannons. It was assigned to the Union blockade. The reason for the name, according to the *New York Herald* on March 31, 1861, was because it was commissioned by Valiente & Company of Cuba and other Cuban shareholders. It was originally meant to be part of a steam line for passengers going from New York to Cuba. The U.S. Navy needed ships for its blockade of the Confederate ports and purchased it for $200,000. It was sent to the Brooklyn Navy Yard on November 5, 1861, and it became part of the East Gulf Blockading Squadron. Its primary mission would be to catch blockade runners between the Gulf Coast and Cuba, as well as later near the Bahamas.

Bazaar was quite busy aboard the ship. Its actions were reported frequently in various newspapers, including the *Connecticut Courant* on May 5, 1862. The newspaper reported that within its first six months out, it captured the Rebel steamer *Isabel* with a valuable cargo of arms, ammunition and other contraband. It was captured after it left Nassau on its way to Charleston, South Carolina, on April 28, 1862. The *Santiago* also captured a Confederate schooner named the *Lucy C. Holmes*. This schooner was loaded with cotton for trade. An added benefit of catching a blockade runner is that the crew got a cut of the goods confiscated. According to Arthur Wyllie in the *Union Navy* on September 1862, the *Santiago* was assigned to the "Flying Squadron." It was created to "capture [the] Confederate commerce raiders Alabama and Florida." They never apprehended them but did apprehend plenty of other blockade runners. The *Santiago* continued its assignment until the vessel was sent to Boston for repairs in December 1863. It remained there until June 1864, when it was sent back to sea. It would eventually be reassigned in late 1864 to the North Atlantic Blockading Squadron, which was commanded by Rear Admiral David Dixon Porter. It was time for the Union navy to close the port at Wilmington, North Carolina.

The Battle of Fort Fisher was fought December 23–27, 1864. This is considered the first assault by Major General Benjamin Frank Butler and Admiral David Dixon Porter on the fort. The goal was to capture Fort Fisher, which guarded Wilmington, North Carolina's last major port. According to the *Records of the War of the Rebellion*, "Wilmington, N.C. was the most important sea-coast port left. They could sell cotton and other cash crops to Europe using blockade-runners." It was also "a place of great strategic value." Admiral Porter wanted to assemble the "most formidable armada ever collected for concentration upon one given point." It was the largest armada in U.S. history until the invasion of Normandy during World War II.

This battle was broken up into two phases. The first Battle of Fort Fisher was more of a siege than an actual battle. It was led by Major General Benjamin Butler. In an attempt to breach the fort, a captured blockade runner, the USS *Louisiana*, was loaded with large amounts of gunpowder on December 23, 1864. General Butler believed that if the ship were pulled in close enough to the fort, it could be detonated, and the explosion would breach the wall. The vessel was believed by S.W. Preston, a lieutenant in the U.S. Navy, in his report, to be some three hundred yards from the fort's walls when it was detonated in the early hours of December 24, 1864. The attempt failed because it was just not close enough to be effective. Still not deterred, it was ordered to shell the fort for two days straight, including Christmas Day. The only effect was to send the Confederate defenders into their bomb shelters.

After two days of almost nonstop shelling, troops were landed to start the Siege of Fort Fisher. It was abandoned when General Butler learned that Confederate reinforcements were marching to the relief of the fort. Finally, the weather was not cooperating either, and the siege had to be lifted. Several prisoners were captured and being held on Bazaar's ship. The 142nd New York Regiment had even captured a Rebel flag and a whole battalion of

Rebel troops outside the fort. Porter became furious in his reports because he felt strongly that the fort could have been taken the first time.

Admiral David Dixon Porter believed that the fort could have been successfully captured if a competent officer had been placed in charge of the operation. In his opinion, Butler was not that man. He maintained that Butler had given up on the siege too easily. Porter told Lieutenant General Grant his feelings, and Grant agreed with the admiral. Grant decided to recall Butler. However, Grant needed the permission of Secretary of War Edwin Stanton or, in his absence, President Lincoln. On January 7, 1865, General Order No. 1 was issued by President Lincoln: "By direction of the President of the United States, Maj. Gen. B.F. Butler is relieved of command of the Department of North Carolina and Virginia. Lt.-General Grant will designate an officer to take his command temporarily." He was replaced by Major General Alfred H. Terry.

Grant wrote to Terry, "The expedition intrusted [*sic*] to your command has been fitted out to renew the attempt to capture Fort Fisher, N.C., and Wilmington ultimately." Fort Fisher contained more than 2,200 men. A second attempt was coming against Fort Fisher, and O.S. Bazaar and the *Santiago de Cuba* would be a part of that attack. Captain Oliver S. Glisson oversaw the *Santiago de Cuba*.

North Carolina Historic Sites, in the article "Such a Hell of Noise," related that on January 12, 1865, Admiral Porter had "58 warships." Upon seeing the ships arriving, Colonel William Lamb, a Confederate officer at the fort, referred to it as a great armada. The following morning, on January 13, 1865, Union gunboats started shelling the "peninsula at a point four miles north of Fort Fisher—the area chosen by Terry as the new Federal landing zone." Shortly after shelling ceased, the amphibious assault started with a landing on the beach. Admiral Porter also sent some of his sailors and marines to help with the assault on the fort, which was slowly being silenced by the massive bombardment of the armada.

According to North Carolina Historic Sites, by midday on January 15, 1865, "the Union fleet has destroyed every gun on the land face of Fort Fisher, with the exception of two 8-inch Columbiads, which is a large caliber cannon capable of firing a 128-pound shell." They could be rifled or smoothbore. This was when Porter's marines and sailors, about two thousand men, went ashore. In the afternoon, the gunships grew silent, and the land invasion of the fort was launched. Philip Bazaar was aboard the USS *Santiago*. He went ashore at midday with the two thousand or so sailors.

According to a report by Lieutenant Farquhar of the U.S. Navy, who was commanding the assaulting party from the *Santiago de Cuba*, the assaulting party consisted of thirty-five sailors and fourteen marines from the *Santiago de Cuba*. He wrote on January 19, 1865, from Norfolk, Virginia, that "on the morning of the 15th, in charge of the landing party of this steamer, consisting of Acting Ensign E.C. Bowers, Acting Master's Mates E.C. Finney and Richard Lyons, 35 sailors, and 14 marines." All reported to Fleet Captain Breese for the assault, and the charge on the fort commenced at 3:00 p.m. "with a cheer and a determination to plant our colors on the ramparts." He reported that the marines and sailors were forced to fall back and, at one point, were left at the base of the fort alone for a few hours. When the fort was eventually breached, Bazaar entered the fort with six other sailors. He carried dispatches between officers at the height of the battle to Major General Terry. Bazaar would be awarded the Medal of Honor for his actions. The fort surrendered on the night of January 15, 1865.

Once the fort fell, the city of Wilmington quickly followed, further cutting off the South from trade with Europe and other countries. After Fort Fisher, the USS *Santiago* returned to Norfolk, Virginia. From here, on January 19, 1865, Bazaar inquired of J.D. Braman, the paymaster general in Massachusetts, to "please send my bounty by Adam's Express to Norfolk, Va.…I am now in the need of it." He signed the letter "Phillip Bazan." The amount he was requesting was $100, "being bounty due for three years enlistment from May 18, 1864." The payment was sent by Adam's Express on January 23, 1865.

The war ended in April 1865, and on June 17, 1865, Bazaar was transferred from the *Santiago de Cuba* to the USS *Princeton*. It was recorded that he never did report for duty. There is no indication that he deserted from the U.S. Navy. There seems to be little indication that he was dishonorably discharged. He was also awarded the Medal of Honor in June 1865. His paperwork in the Massachusetts Archives recorded, "possibly deserted."

Where Bazaar was from January 1865 to the 1880s is not known. Did he return to Chile or was he out at sea? He is listed later in life as a seaman. Eventually, he did end up settling in New York City, where numerous census and directories list him as a seaman and having different residences during that same period. For example, according to *Trow's New York City Directory* for 1893–1894, he was living at 129 Monroe Street and listed as a seaman. In the same directory for 1894–96, he was living on 3rd Avenue, where he was listed not as a seaman but as a machinist.

Philip Bazaar eventually married an Irish immigrant named Bridget Ford in 1888. She was born on January 7, 1851. Her family had come to the United States in 1852, presumably during the Great Famine. Prior to her marriage, Bridget worked as a rope maker in a factory in New York City according to the 1870 federal census. However, she lived in Brooklyn prior to relocating to Manhattan. Just prior to marrying Philip, she was an "operator on shirts."

Philip and Bridget, as far as we can ascertain, did not have any children who lived to adulthood. They lived at various locations around New York City, including with Bridget's widowed sister, Ellen Wade, in 1910. By 1910, Philip was being listed as a retired seaman. The last census he was recorded in was in 1915, and one of the people listed in the household was Agnes Bazan, who would have been his niece. Two years later, according to a New York City directory for that same year, he lived at 49 East 90th Street. His wife, Bridget, had died in New York City two years before, on December 7, 1913. According to her death certificate, she died of a heart attack at the family home.

Philip passed away on December 28, 1923. His death certificate, filed in New York City, stated that he had no family. The death certificate listed his last address as 49 East 90th Street. Two days later, he was buried at Cavalry Cemetery in Woodside, Queens. There is currently no headstone. His age at the time of his death was seventy-eight.

David Glasgow Farragut

Damn the torpedoes! Full speed ahead!

—*Admiral Farragut*

Woodlawn Cemetery, which is located in the Bronx just outside New York City, holds the remains of many notable individuals in U.S. history. The cemetery was founded in 1863 and is situated on four hundred acres of parklike land. It was created for a Manhattan elite who was rapidly running out of burial space on Manhattan Island. Woodlawn was a short enough distance away that people could travel from Manhattan to visit their loved ones. Located in Lot no. 1429-44, Section 14, on a high point in the cemetery is Aurora Point. The remains of Admiral David Glasgow Farragut and his family are located here. This marble and granite sculpture was erected after his death to memorialize his life. It was commissioned by his wife, Virginia, and son, Loyall. The monument serves to commemorate, in stone, the highlights of David Farragut's momentous life. It is unfortunate that the first admiral, first vice-admiral and first four-star admiral in U.S. Navy history has been somewhat forgotten.

When Admiral Farragut is remembered, it is usually for an utterance during the Battle of Mobile Bay on August 5, 1864. During this Civil War battle, it was discovered that Mobile Bay was booby-trapped with mines, or torpedoes as they were called at the time. Faced with the decision to abandon the attack or continue forward, Farragut proclaimed, "Damn the torpedoes! Full speed ahead!" However, this man of Hispanic heritage was so much more than these six words. He was perhaps one of the most respected military men of his time, and his flagship, the USS *Hartford*, was the most feared.

David Glasgow Farragut was born James Glasgow Farragut on July 5, 1801, in Campbell's Station, Tennessee. He was born to a Spanish immigrant named Jordi Farragut Mesquida and his North Carolina–born wife, Elizabeth Shine. According to *The Life of David Glasgow Farragut*, written by his son, Loyall Farragut, Jordi was born on September 29, 1755, on the Island of Minorca, which was part of Spain and located in the Mediterranean Sea. The town he lived in was Ciudadela, which is located on the western part of the island. According to the family Bible, Jordi decided to leave the island on April 2, 1772.

The family had sent Jordi, nicknamed Jorge, to Barcelona at about ten years of age for what they felt would be a proper education. Against his family's wishes, Jordi left Barcelona without permission and went to sea aboard a merchant ship. Loyall wrote that he was "plying the trade routes of the Mediterranean." Jordi eventually became a merchant ship's captain and sailed to New Orleans in 1775, then a colony of Spain. Farragut commanded a Spanish cargo ship that traded between Havana, Cuba, Veracruz, Mexico and New Orleans. James Duffy, in his book *Lincoln's Admiral*, wrote that Jordi joined the cause of the Patriots during the American Revolution by supplying them. Eventually, he was commissioned as a first lieutenant in the South Carolina navy. The Battlefield Trust states that he is "the only known Spanish volunteer who fought under the American flag in the Revolutionary War."

Jordi had extensive experience on the sea. He used that experience in the defense of Savannah and later the Siege of Charlestown. During the siege, he was the commander of a battery. When the siege broke on May 12, 1780, General Sir Henry Clinton took as prisoner some five thousand American prisoners. During the siege, Farragut was wounded. His right arm was shattered by either a cannonball or a musket ball. Russell Shorto, in his book *David Farragut and the Great Naval Blockade*, wrote that Farragut escaped while being held prisoner. Duffy noted that he could not be kept out of the fight for long. Farragut became a privateer sailing out of Philadelphia. Lieutenant Farragut, who had changed his name to George by this time, eventually joined the Continental cavalry in North Carolina, attaining the rank of major. He is known to have participated in the Battles of Cowpens and Wilmington.

David Glasgow Farragut, circa 1862. *National Portrait Gallery.*

Once the war ended, George continued to do what he knew and loved best: plying the seas for trade. There was money to be made in what was then called the West Indies. In 1795, he met Elizabeth Shine and married her. He temporarily relocated to Knoxville, Tennessee, where his first son, William Augustus Claiborne Farragut, was born in 1797. On July 5, 1801, a second son was born at Campbell Station, Tennessee, where the family had relocated. This second child was named James Glasgow Farragut. When James was six years old, the family moved again, this time to New Orleans. It was here that David Farragut's life would be changed forever.

William Charles Cole Claiborne was a family friend who later became governor of Orleans Territory. This later became the state of Louisiana. After the purchase of Louisiana by the United States, Claiborne asked George to relocate to New Orleans in 1807. He was made a sailing master as well as a commander of a gunboat. A gunboat was a "small" ship used during the war. It could be rowed or powered by sails. A gunboat was not

George Farragut.
*Smithsonian Institute,
Naval History
Division.*

considered heavily armed. George patrolled the Mississippi River. In New Orleans, events would change the destiny of the Farragut family.

In "A Long-Lost Farragut Letter Is Rediscovered," the author, John B. Hattendorf, quoted from a letter written by Farragut about his early life. "He did not know much about his father, that he only remembered his father in Tennessee and as a farmer and soldier." He was only five years old when they moved to New Orleans. He did remember that his father's associates called him major. One of the family's friends was Sailing Master David Porter Sr.

Sailing Master David Porter Sr. was originally from Massachusetts. Like George, he served in the American Revolution. Porter, in 1808, was fifty-four years old and in poor health. One of his favorite pastimes was fishing on Lake Pontchartrain, where he also had a home. The story told by the Farragut family is that while Porter was fishing, he succumbed to sunstroke. Coincidentally, George Farragut was also fishing on the lake when he happened upon Porter unconscious in his boat. George brought the man back to his home, where Elizabeth did her best to nurse Porter back to health. They later found out that Porter was also suffering from what was termed consumption. Today, we would call this tuberculous.

David Porter Sr. died on June 22, 1808. In a tragic twist of fate, Elizabeth Farragut contracted yellow fever and, while nursing Porter, became sick herself. Elizabeth died the same day as Porter. James Farragut wrote years later that he "knew nothing of the sickness of my mother until she had been dead some time." Shortly after their deaths, David Porter Jr. was alerted that his father had passed away. Porter Jr. was an officer in the U.S. Navy. When he heard of how the Farragut family were so kind to his father, he made it a point to thank the Farragut family in person. Porter Jr. realized that the family were still reeling from the death of Elizabeth.

George made his money on the sea. When Porter Jr. found that Elizabeth had died, it left George responsible for caring for his children. The other children still living at home, along with James of course, were George Anthony Farragut, born in 1805; Nancy Anne Shine Farragut, born in 1804; and Elizabeth Farragut, born in 1807. George found guardians for all the children except James. William, the oldest, who had been born in 1797, was constantly away at sea. He was a midshipman in the U.S. Navy. Hearing about the dilemma facing George, Porter offered to take James as an apprentice at sea. Farragut wrote in the same letter found by Hattendorf that the junior Porter "had just married and had no children." In addition to James, a sister went with Porter. This allowed his father to resume his seafaring activities. David Porter Jr. continued to live with his family in

New Orleans, allowing the Farragut family to remain in touch. The last time James, who started to refer to himself as David in honor of his new guardian, would see his father was June 1810, when David Porter Jr. was relocated by the navy to Washington, D.C.

Once transferred to the capital, Porter enrolled James in a local school. His sister was left behind in New Orleans with Porter's sister, who had married into a local surgeon's family. The Porters did not stay in Washington, D.C., for an extended period of time. They relocated to Chester, Pennsylvania. Porter was then "ordered to take care of the Frigate Essex." A frigate was a lightly armed but very maneuverable ship. While in Washington, D.C., Porter introduced David Farragut to Secretary of the Navy Paul Hamilton. The secretary observed how David Farragut loved the sea. The secretary promised the young boy that he would commission him a midshipman when he turned ten. He would be a midshipman at nine and a half years old on December 17, 1810. David Farragut served on the USS *Essex* during the War of 1812 with his adopted father.

David continued to advance in rank, becoming a prize master at age eleven. A prize master was an officer placed in charge of a captured vessel. This was the HMS *Albert*, captured on August 13, 1812. Farragut saw plenty of action on the *Essex*, attacking British whaling ships. On March 28, 1814, the *Essex* and its sister ship, *Essex Junior*, were outgunned by the HMS *Phoebe* and sloop *Cherub* off the coast of Chile in the Battle of Valparaiso Bay. The crews of both U.S. ships were taken prisoner. Farragut wrote in his journal, "I was so mortified at our capture that I could not refrain from tears." Once the *Essex Junior* was disarmed, Farragut, Porter and the crew were sent to New York. The War of 1812 was over for Farragut. The Treaty of Ghent ended the war in December 1814.

Commodore David Porter and Farragut would part ways after the war. The man he considered his stepfather would be sent to Washington, D.C., as a naval commissioner. Midshipman Farragut was sent to the Mediterranean after President Madison declared war on Algeria in the Second Barbary War. By the time Farragut entered the Mediterranean, the war was over. This journey marked the first time Farragut was on his own, stationed aboard a ship of the line from 1816 to 1818. The ship of the line was a powerful battleship with heavy guns on two decks.

In the spring of 1816, Farragut was placed on the warship USS *Washington*. The ship was commanded by Captain Creighton. Although Farragut did not make it in time to participate in the Second Barbary War, he did patrol the Mediterranean Sea. During this time, the ship's

David Dixon Porter Jr. *National Portrait Gallery.*

chaplain, Charles Folsom, befriended him. David had not received any consistent formal schooling, which Folsom felt was lacking. Folsom took the midshipman under his care, instructing Farragut in language, history and mathematics. It was also during this time, June 4, 1817, that his biological father died. He continued with his studies and did not try to be at his father's funeral.

Unfortunately, Farragut's studies were jeopardized when Folsom was appointed American consul for the Barbary Coast in Tunis. David requested and received permission to accompany Folsom in order to continue his studies. Traveling with the chaplain enabled Farragut to visit ancient ruins and continue his classical education. David Farragut was not used to the intense heat of the region. During one of his excursions with Folsom, he succumbed to what Loyall later referred to as "stroke from the sun." It would affect his father's eyesight and health for the remainder of his life.

Early in 1819, Farragut was back cruising the Mediterranean, this time aboard the USS *Franklin*. His next commission also came in 1819, as acting lieutenant at eighteen years old. The following year, he returned to the United States. He met his future wife, Susan Marchant, in Norfolk, Virginia, and started to court her. If he wanted to marry her, it would need to wait because he was shipped out in May 1822, this time to the Caribbean. A squadron was created by Commodore David Porter called the Mosquito Fleet. According to Duffy, he was also reunited with his older brother Lieutenant William Farragut. The fleet's job was to rid the Caribbean of piracy, which affected U.S. shipping interests. This mission would last two years.

Shortly after returning to Norfolk, Susan and David were wed on September 2, 1824. After their marriage, they visited Commodore Porter, who was once again living in Washington, D.C. After their visit, the couple made Norfolk, Virginia, their permanent home. He continued to climb the chain of command. In 1825, he was officially promoted to lieutenant after passing the exam. By all accounts, the couple was very happy. David was devoted to Susan, and he watched with concern as her health deteriorated by May 1826. It is believed that she was suffering from neuralgia, which at times was debilitating and painful. Due to his wife's illness, he requested a leave of absence. David wanted answers for his wife's illness. He traveled to Yale College, and then to Philadelphia, to talk to experts who believed they could help Susan. When she seemed as if she might recover, the sea called him away. This time, a looming crisis between the federal government and South Carolina sent him to Charleston, South Carolina.

Lieutenant Farragut played a part in what is known as the Nullification Crisis. This crisis was a sectional dispute in which South Carolina confronted the federal government over the tariffs of 1828 and 1832. South Carolina believed that the tariffs were unfair and unconstitutional. The state declared the right to ignore the tariffs and not enforce them. In addition, South Carolina threatened to secede from the Union. President Andrew Jackson and Congress decided to send warships to Charleston to assert the authority of the federal government. First Lieutenant Farragut, aboard the USS *Natchez*, sailed to Charleston. A compromise was reached, and armed conflict averted.

Alfred T. Mahan, in his 1895 book *Admiral Farragut*, wrote about the period of Farragut's life from 1825 to 1841, "after the terminating of the cruise in the Mosquito Fleet, and up to the beginning of the Civil War, the story of Farragut's life…is routine service of a naval officer in times of peace." Monumental periods still influenced his later career, including a deployment when he was placed in command of the sloop of war *Erie*. He sailed for the east coast of Mexico to protect American property and interests, as Mexico and France were at war. It was a routine deployment. What was not routine was when French Admiral Boudin attacked Veracruz, which was heavily fortified. The bombardment by the French became a study of artillery for Farragut, one he would use later in life. He saw firsthand the effects of different shells on the fortification. Some were more effective than others.

Tragedy struck on December 27, 1840, when Susan Farragut succumbed to her illness. Farragut sought comfort in the sea. Shortly after her death, he was placed in command of the ship USS *Delaware*, which departed Norfolk for Brazil. In 1841, he attained the rank of commander. He was not supposed to be in command of the ship, but Commander Henry Ogden became ill. Farragut was forty years old. Almost three years after Susan died, David Farragut married Virginia Dorcas Loyall. The couple welcomed their first child on October 12, 1844. He was named Loyall Farragut.

On May 13, 1846, Congress declared war on Mexico due to the deaths of U.S. soldiers on what was claimed as American soil. Mexico claimed that the border between Texas and Mexico was the Nueces River, while the United States believed it was the Rio Grande. President Polk sent General Zachary Taylor to patrol the area claimed by the United States. Mexico launched an attack on the soldiers. America was spreading its influence west using Manifest Destiny as a pretext. On March 29, 1847, Commander Farragut, aboard the sloop of war *Saratoga*, left Norfolk for the Gulf of Mexico. He hoped for a large role in the war, stating in letters to Secretary of War William Learned Marcy that he had been to that area in 1838 when Veracruz had been attacked by the French. He believed that the castle that guarded the entrance to the harbor where Veracruz stood could be taken using his battle plan. His letters went unanswered. Much to Farragut's disappointment, General Winfield Scott had already completed the task when he was finally sent to Veracruz. Farragut ended up being part of the Tuxpan blockade. He did not receive any glory, only a severe case of yellow fever that almost took his life. Farragut was later sent back to the United States, where he was appointed assistant inspector of ordnance at Norfolk until 1853.

The same year, Farragut was reassigned by Secretary of the Navy James C. Dobbin to California. Dobbins requested that Farragut create a naval base on Mare Island near San Francisco, to be the first U.S. naval base on the West Coast. It took Farragut four years to create the base. During his

David Glasgow Farragut as a young man. *National Portrait Gallery*.

time out there, he was promoted to captain on September 14, 1855. Two years later, he returned to the East Coast and was placed in command of the sloop of war *Brooklyn*, patrolling the Gulf of Mexico and returning to Norfolk in 1859.

Abraham Lincoln was elected president of the United States in November 1860. South Carolina became the first state to secede from the Union on December 20, 1860. Once it became apparent to Captain Farragut that the country was moving toward Civil War, he hoped that Virginia would remain loyal to the Union. His son wrote about the quandary his father faced with his allegiance. Loyall wrote that navy men would meet in Norfolk at "a certain store and talk over the news of the day every morning." Captain Farragut made it clear to the other officers that his first allegiance was with the U.S. government. He stated, according to his son, "God forbid I should have to raise my hand against the South." However, if he had to do it, he would do it. Once Virginia declared its intentions to leave the Union, he discussed it at the store. He was told that he could not live in Norfolk if he were siding with Lincoln. He accepted this. He disagreed with secession and saw it as an act of treason. However, he waited to see if Virginia would actually leave the Union. Virginia decided to secede in April 1861. David Farragut discussed the situation with his wife, Virginia. She came from an old prominent southern family. Farragut understood how this would tear the country and families apart. In the end, she decided to stay with her husband and child. The same evening that the State of Virginia voted to leave the Union, the family boarded a steamer for Baltimore, Maryland. They then secured a canalboat to New York City. Loyall remembered that they stayed in New York City for a few days, and from New York City, they went north to Hastings-on-the-Hudson. This was a small village in New York's Lower Hudson Valley.

According to the Historical Society of Hastings, in a blog written in 2009, "[Loyall] lived there for barely five years, and for most of that time Farragut himself was at sea." They lived at 60 Main Street and, at some point, also rented a two-family cottage at the corner of "Washington Avenue and Broadway." The family rented half the cottage. While in Hastings, Farragut awaited his next assignment. The federal government was still not sure about its Southern officers. They needed time to figure out who was loyal and who was not. Mahan wrote that many Southerners in the military service for the Union did not want to fight against the South. "Men were heard to say that they would not go with their state, but neither would they fight against her."

Farragut did request to command a fleet to search for the CSA *Sumter*, "the first of the Confederate cruisers." He was not granted the assignment. Instead, he was given an assignment in Brooklyn as a retiring board member. The board met to recommend officers who were being considered for retirement. This was in 1861. His time of waiting was coming to an end.

Virginia Farragut. *Naval History and Heritage Command.*

The appointment he craved was on the horizon. It was frustrating for David Farragut, who wanted to serve his country. He would be tested before he was given an appointment.

In 1861, General Winfield Scott was the commanding general of the United States. He had held that position since July 5, 1841. His Union

Captain Farragut. *Naval History and Heritage Command.*

strategy was to capture the Mississippi River, splitting the Confederacy in two. In addition, Scott wanted to create a complete blockade of Southern ports, which, given the state of the U.S. Navy, must have seemed impossible. The press dubbed this the "Anaconda Plan" because, like the snake, it would slowly strangle the South, most notably preventing the South from selling its valuable cotton to Europe. In order to continue trade, the South would have to resort to blockade runners. These blockade runners would bring valuable supplies to the Southern war effort.

One of the most troubling areas of the blockade was the Gulf of Mexico. Winfield Scott wanted to deny the South's use of the Mississippi River. Duffy wrote that Scott wanted to "use between 60,000 and 80,000 soldiers stationed along the Mississippi River from Cairo, Illinois, to the Gulf Coast to close that river to enemy use." This task was enormous. The navy might be a better option, some reasoned. Gideon Welles, who became the secretary of the navy because of his loyalty to Abraham Lincoln in the 1860 elections, developed the navy into a force capable of executing the blockade. He would accomplish this goal with the help of his assistant secretary of the navy, Gustavus Fox. The priority became capturing the South's most populous city, New Orleans, which lay at the mouth of the Mississippi.

The South, knowing the importance of its most populous city, had undertaken efforts to fortify the approaches from the Gulf of Mexico and north of New Orleans. A leader needed to be selected for the task. According to Loyall Farragut, Secretary Welles claimed that he knew Farragut and respected him. He reported that he was the one who eventually selected Farragut as the flag officer for the Western Blockade Squadron. He rightly asserted that Joseph Smith, who was a master commandant, endorsed Farragut. The reason was that Smith, who had been in the navy for five decades, did not push for the position for himself. He was content as the chief of the Bureau of Yards and Docks, a position he had held since the 1840s. It was agreed that Farragut would be a good choice. Once again, Farragut's loyalty would need to be tested though.

Once the decision was made, Commander David Dixon Porter, Farragut's stepbrother, was tasked with the mission to ascertain Farragut's loyalty. When meeting with Farragut, Porter created a hypothetical situation. He told Farragut that he was given orders to attack Norfolk, Virginia. Watching his stepbrother for any reaction, Porter asked Farragut if he felt comfortable with the assignment. Farragut balked at the possibility of attacking his "hometown." He thought about what Porter was asking him. After what must have been like an eternity, Farragut replied that he would take the assignment. Only then did Porter tell Farragut that the intended target was actually New Orleans. Farragut must have been somewhat relieved. However, he still had family living in that city.

His orders arrived from the Navy Department on January 9, 1862. Gideon Welles instructed Farragut that he would be appointed commander of the Western Gulf Blockading Squadron. His ship would be the USS *Hartford*, which was currently being constructed in Philadelphia. It was a sloop of war, meant to be his flagship. The confidential orders, according to Loyall, demanded the "reduction of the defenses guarding the approaches to New Orleans and the taking possession of that city." He was also to enforce the blockade in the Western Gulf of Mexico. When asked if he believed he could carry out these orders, he felt he could accomplish it. While waiting for the flagship to be built, Farragut moved to Philadelphia with his family. He left Philadelphia aboard the *Hartford* on January 23, 1862. Just shy of a month later, Farragut arrived at Ship Island, Mississippi.

While at Ship Island, the Western Gulf Blockading Squadron enforced the blockade while it planned an attack on New Orleans. Intelligence needed to be gathered about the area. According to Duffy, on March 18, 1862, Farragut sent a raiding party into Biloxi, Mississippi, to search the local post office for copies of local newspapers. Farragut wanted to know what was being said about the war effort and any other information he could gather from the newspapers. This same day, the fleet assembled and made ready to start the attack plan on the Mississippi River. When assembled, according to Kevin J. Dougherty and John D. Wright in *The Civil War: A Military History*, Farragut would have command of "24 wooden vessels, 19 mortar boats and a support army of 15,000."

Subduing the Mississippi would be a formidable task. One of the obstacles in ascending the Mississippi from the South was the constantly shifting sandbars of the delta, which could easily trap a boat. Even warships like the *Hartford*, which had both sails and steam power, struggled with the formidable current of the Mississippi. In addition, there were two forts hoping to sink any ships that made it up the Mississippi. Fort St. Philip was on the left bank of the river, and a little farther down the river on the right was Fort Jackson. Near the forts were sunken boats and a chain to snare enemy boats. New Orleans was on the left bank of the river, "about one hundred miles from its mouth." If this were not enough, according to Loyall, using his father's papers, "a river fleet of fifteen vessels, under Confederate Commodore J.K. Mitchell, including the iron-clad ram Manassas and an immense floating battery covered with railroad iron called the Louisiana." This fleet was known as the River Defense Fleet. It also included dreaded fire rafts. These rafts instilled fear in sailors on wooden ships. Finally, the Confederates had about four thousand soldiers defending the river, and this included sharpshooters on both sides of the Mississippi. The Confederates were expecting an attack from the North, believing that an attack from the South was near impossible.

It was decided that the best approach would be from the South. Porter believed that the twin forts could be bombed into submission with a two-day mortar blitz. An obstacle that needed to be overcome was the tight bend in the river where the forts were situated. The flotilla would be like sitting ducks when it slowed down to navigate the turn. They would also need to figure out a way to make it past the river obstructions. Loyall wrote, "It was the most powerful naval expedition that had ever sailed under the American flag." It was believed that once they secured the surrender of New Orleans, General B.F. Butler would be able to hold the city.

On April 18, 1862, Porter commenced his bombardment of the forts. His bombardment did not achieve its goal. On April 20, 1862, Farragut held a meeting aboard the *Hartford*. Clearly, the mortar bombardment was not working. Ammunition was also running low. Based on his studies of bombardment, Farragut never believed that this plan was destined to work. He felt that sailing directly past the forts was the best course of action. The forts would be effectively cut off once they made it to New Orleans. The only officer not present at the meeting aboard the flagship was Porter. However, he still made his feelings known to Farragut that given more time, the bombardment would work. Farragut decided that the best course of action would be to chance pushing up the Mississippi past the forts. Four days later, Farragut, under the cover of darkness, attempted to make it past the forts. They successfully broke through the chain. According to Russell Shorto, this was accomplished by Captain Henry Bell. Once above the forts, they were met by the Confederate ironclads *Manassas* and *Louisiana*, as well as fire boats.

New Orleans fell to the fleet on April 25, 1862. Farragut sent a force onshore to hoist the U.S. flag over all public buildings. Afterward, General Butler took control of New Orleans when it formally surrendered after trying to hold out. Theodorus Bailey, second in command of the attack, wrote to senior officers at Key West, "We fought two great battles; that of the passage of the forts and encounter with the ironclads and gunboats has not been surpassed in naval history. We have done all this with wooden ships and gunboats. All honor and an admiral's commission for Flag-officer Farragut." They only lost one vessel, the USS *Varuna*.

Farragut took time after the fall of the city to write a letter to his wife and son. It started with, "My Dearest Wife and Boy: I am so agitated that I can scarcely write; and shall only tell you that it has pleased Almighty God to preserve my life a fire such as the world has scarcely seen." On April 29, 1862, aboard the *Hartford*, "at anchor off the city of New Orleans," Farragut wrote to Welles, "Sir: I can happily announce to you that our flag waves over both Forts Jackson and St. Philip, and at the New Orleans Custom House. I am taking every means to secure the occupation by General Butler of all the forts along the coast."

After the capture of New Orleans, Farragut sent a vessel up the Mississippi River under the command of Captain Craven. Farragut wrote, "The large ships; I fear, will not be able to go higher than Baton Rouge." The fleet took Baton Rouge on May 9 and Natchez, Mississippi, on May 12, 1862. Commander S. Phillips Lee reached Vicksburg by May 18, 1862. He demanded the surrender of Vicksburg, but the city refused. A Union force was driving south down the river at the time under Flag Officer Charles H. Davis. According to Matt Atkinson, they captured "Island No.10 on April 8 and Memphis on June 6, 1862," noted in an article for the *Mississippi Encyclopedia*. When Memphis fell, the only portions of the river not in control of the Union were Port Hudson and Vicksburg.

Farragut was making his way toward Lee's forces. He finally made it to Vicksburg three days later. He decided to leave a small group of boats, but the large attack did not happen. Farragut was questioned as to why he did not continue up to Vicksburg and attack it. In his defense, he wrote that it was not because he could not take it or get past it. He was advised by his captains, while he was sick, that once past the fort, they would be cut off from coal and other supplies. He also saw that not only was the Mississippi a dangerous place for large oceangoing vessels that far up the river, but in the summer, water levels would also drop dangerously low for large ships. They could become stranded until the water level rose again. Farragut ordered the larger vessels back to New Orleans.

When Secretary of War Welles and President Lincoln received word of this move, they ordered Farragut to bring his whole fleet up to Vicksburg. One month later, on June 25, 1862, he was back and ordered a bombardment of Vicksburg that would last until June 28. Some of the fleet of smaller ships managed to move past Vicksburg and met with Davis's arriving fleet on July 1, 1862. Roughly two weeks later, Farragut was commissioned the first rear admiral of the U.S. Navy as a reward for taking New Orleans. Prior to this, the navy did not rank above captain. According to the navy, "Many people felt the title too reminiscent of royalty to be used in the republic's navy." It was this way until 1862, when Farragut was commissioned.

The attack on Vicksburg proved unsuccessful. Because of the falling water levels and dwindling supplies, Farragut was forced to send his fleet back down the river. Vicksburg would not fall until July 4, 1863, after a long siege of more than forty days. It would be with the help of the Western Gulf Blockading Squadron that Grant would be successful in capturing both Vicksburg and Port Hudson, which were supplied by goods moving along the Red River.

After Vicksburg, Farragut turned his attention to Mobile Bay in Alabama. It is also the battle for which he perhaps is most well known. The day before the battle, aboard the flagship *Hartford*, Farragut wrote a letter to his wife, Virginia, back in Hastings-on-the-Hudson. "My dearest Wife, I write and leave this letter for you. I am going into Mobile Bay in the morning if 'God is my leader' as I hope he is, and in him, I place my trust if he thinks it is the proper place for me to die." The battle started on August 5 and ended on August 23. Farragut would succeed in controlling the entire Gulf of Mexico. He also closed a valuable port for blockade runners.

The challenge was the three forts that guarded the bay: Forts Morgan, Powell and Gaines. In addition to the forts, the waterway was booby-trapped with torpedoes. Finally, the forts were supported by an ironclad, the CSS *Tennessee*, as well as gunboats. Farragut would be in charge of the naval support; Union ironclads and wooden ships entered the bay in support of Major General Gordon Granger, who was to attack the forts by land.

On August 5, 1864, Farragut, with Union ironclads and wooden ships, entered the bay. Farragut lashed himself to the rigging of the *Hartford* so he could observe the battle. When the USS *Tecumseh* struck a torpedo, it quickly sank. Farragut asked why the ships were stopping or turning around. He was told that the waterway had torpedoes blocking their way. His response was, "Damn the torpedoes! Full speed ahead!" Three hours later, Farragut defeated the Confederate navy and controlled the port. The forts eventually capitulated—Fort Powell on August 5, Fort Gaines on August 8 and Fort Morgan on August 23. Without supplies, their situation was hopeless.

After the battle, accolades poured in from Washington, D.C. President Lincoln wrote on September 3, 1864, "The national thanks are tendered by the President to Admiral Farragut and Major-General Canby for the skill and harmony with which the recent operations in Mobile Harbor and against Fort Powell, Fort Gaines, and Fort Morgan." In another letter, he ordered a one-hundred-gun salute on September 5 at noon at the arsenal at Washington, D.C., and every navy yard. In another letter, the president proclaimed a day of fasting. A broken and exhausted Farragut penned a letter on August 27, 1864, asking for a break of active duty. In a letter to Farragut, Duffy wrote that Welles wanted him to head to North Carolina to take Fort Fisher. In a letter by Farragut, he wrote, "I fear my health is giving way." He had been in the Gulf and Caribbean for "nearly five out of six years." He had a short stay home the previous last fall but wrote to Welles, "I want a rest if it is to be had."

Battle of Mobile Bay. *Naval History and Heritage Command.*

According to Mahan, Farragut left the squadron under the control of Commodore James S. Palmer. The *New York Times* followed Farragut closely with the December 14 arrival of the USS *Hartford* in New York City. Farragut had traveled from Pensacola on November 30 to Key West on December 5 before arriving in New York City. When he arrived, he was given a New York greeting on board his flagship. He had a warm reception at the customhouse. He became the nation's first vice-admiral on December 21, 1864. On January 1, 1865, he was gifted $50,000 from the public as a token of gratitude for his service in the Civil War. They also hoped he would use it to buy a home and settle in New York City.

The following year, on April 14, 1865, Lee surrendered to Grant at Appomattox Courthouse. Sadly, five days later, President Abraham Lincoln was shot and killed at Ford's Theatre. Farragut was chosen as a pallbearer for the fallen president. Andrew Johnson became the new president. That summer, on July 25, 1866, Farragut was commissioned an admiral, again a first for the nation. He was then given command of the European Squadron with a new flagship, the USS *Franklin*. According to Mahan, he left New York City on June 28, 1867, and arrived in France on July 14, 1867. During his European tour, he visited the island of Minorca, where his family originated, including Ciudadela, where his late father had been born. He sailed back to New York City, arriving on November 10, 1868. His tour would continue to California in 1869, where he visited the California coast, specifically Mare Island, which he had helped create about ten years earlier.

According to Duffy, Admiral Farragut suffered several heart attacks over the years. He celebrated what would be his last birthday on July 5, 1870. Admiral Farragut inspected the Portsmouth Navy Yard in New Hampshire with Commodore Alexander M. Pennock. While there, the admiral suffered a stroke on August 14, 1870. He died at noon at the residence of Pennock. September 30 was declared a holiday. Schools, banks and businesses were closed. There was also a large military funeral procession. In Washington, D.C., a statue of Farragut was erected; today, it is known as Farragut Square. He was interred at Woodlawn Cemetery in the Bronx.

Federico and Adolfo Cavada

Adiós Cuba, para siempre.

—*Federico Cavada*

Isidoro Fernández Cavada was born in Santander, Spain. He went to Cuba, where he met and married Emily Howard Gatier, a U.S. citizen from Philadelphia, Pennsylvania. The couple would have three sons: Emilio, born on October 25, 1830; Federico, born on July 8, 1831; and Adolphus, born on May 17, 1832. They were all born in Cienfuegos, Cuba, and would have a lifelong attachment to the island. If their father had not died in 1838, it is safe to assume that all three brothers would have spent the rest of their lives in Cuba. Jesse Alemán, in her chapter "From Union Officers to Cuban Rebels," wrote that Emily taught for a short amount of time in Cuba after her husband died. For reasons unstated, their mother decided to leave Cuba with her three sons. She returned to Philadelphia, where she had family. According to Dr. Antonio Rafael de la Cova, the family arrived on July 28, 1841, on the brig *Delaware*. They would eventually reside at 222 Spruce Street in Philadelphia.

Little is known about the early lives of two of the brothers, Adolphus and Federico. We know a little bit more about Federico because of works written by him and about him by friends after his death. The best attempt is piecing together scattered documents that survive about Adolphus and Federico. Once the family arrived in the United States, all three brothers were briefly enrolled in boarding school in Wilmington, Delaware.

However, they were eventually enrolled in Philadelphia's Central High School. According to the school archives, the Central High School of Philadelphia is "the second oldest continuous public school in the United States. It was chartered in 1836 as an all-boys school." Federico would have attended school in the earliest school building at Juniper and Mark Streets. "His class would've been the 15th class," according to the archivist for the school. Adolphus was in the twenty-third class. There is no other information on Adolphus or even his early life. "There were two classes per year, finishing in January and finishing in June." Federico graduated in 1850. The school mainly educated middle-class students. It offered careers that would be seen as benefiting society. The course of study were mostly art, math, science, engineering and drawing. Federico excelled at his studies in sketching and engineering. When he graduated, John C. Trautwine, a native of Philadelphia, asked him to join a surveying exhibition in Panama to build a railroad that would eventually cross the isthmus. Trautwine was a civil engineer well known for his railroad work.

Before the transcontinental railroad spanned the United States, the way to travel across the country to the gold fields of California was by crossing the country by foot or horse, which was fraught with dangers. It also took almost half a year or longer to accomplish this journey. Another way to travel was around the tip of South America and up the West Coast from the Atlantic Ocean to the Pacific Ocean. A railroad was sorely needed. According to *Harper's New Monthly Magazine*, in 1849, George Totten and John C. Trautwine were skillful, successful civil engineers. Totten was the chief engineer in the construction of the Panama Railroad.

When Mr. Trautwine started to survey for a railroad in 1850, he asked Federico, who had just graduated, to join as a surveyor. This was no easy feat, as *Harper's* recorded that mosquitos "prove[d] so annoying to the laborers that, unless their faces were protected by gauze veil, no work could be done, even at midday." Many men contracted diseases, such as malaria, which killed many workers. The Pacific and Atlantic Oceans finally met on the "27th day of January 1855, at midnight, in darkness and rain." On the twenty-eighth, a "locomotive passed from Ocean to Ocean." By the time Federico returned from his trip to the Isthmus of Panama, his health was broken, and he made it a goal to recover. Roughly the same year that Federico returned from the isthmus, he applied to become a citizen of the United States. This would not be granted until 1865.

Federico married Carmela Merino de Fernández Cavada sometime in the 1850s. During this time, his only child, Samuel, was born. There is little information about the life of his wife or son. The *International Genealogical Index* notes that Federico was married in Cuba in 1855. His son, Samuel, was born in 1856. However, by the 1860 federal census, his name was misspelled as "F.F. Cabada," and his occupation was listed as merchant. In the same census, Federico and Adolphus's mother was now married to a coal dealer named Samuel Dutton. His mother and close family and friends did not call the two brothers by their formal names. Federico was known as Frederick, or Fred for short. Adolphus was simply Adolfo.

When Fort Sumter was attacked in April 1861, igniting the Civil War, President Abraham Lincoln called for seventy-five thousand volunteers from the states; they were asked to serve for three months. Fred and his brother were known to be antislavery. They decided to join for three months. The federal government, along with many citizens, was very naïve and felt that this was about how long the war would probably last. When it comes to Adolfo and Fred, their military service at the beginning of the war can be confusing. If we turn to the Pennsylvania Archives and look at Adolfo's diary, which was kept from 1861 to 1865, he joined the Union cause earlier than his brother. Perhaps Fred's mother begged him not to enlist because she felt his health was still so fragile from his time in Panama—he had likely contracted malaria.

Adolfo did not initially join the 23rd Regiment, as some publications insist. Instead, he enlisted as a private in the Commonwealth Heavy Artillery for three months. He was mustered into service of the United States on April 19, 1861. Four days later, as he recorded in his diary, he was ordered to Fort Delaware and remained there until his three months of service were completed. Private Cavada noted that while there, they "mounted 56 heavy guns and placed the fort in a good state of defense." The Heavy Artillery returned to Philadelphia on July 30, 1861. There was a public reception. He wrote again in his diary that it was "both civic and military." On August 1, 1861, Adolfo received his pay and was mustered out of service. On August 5, 1861, he was appointed a first lieutenant of the 23rd Regiment, Pennsylvania Volunteers. Lieutenant Colonel D.B. Birney had authorized him to raise his own company. Once this was accomplished, First Lieutenant Cavada was commissioned as a captain in Company C.

During this time, on August 6, 1861, his older brother decided to go against his family's protests. Fred enlisted in the 23rd Regiment as well. He was appointed a captain in Company K. However, this did not last long, for eventually, he was detached because of his experience as an engineer. During the Peninsula Campaign in 1862, he was part of the Balloon Corps. These balloons were like modern-day spy satellites. They were used as spotters for artillery. According to the National Park Service in the article "Air Ballons in the Civil War," the balloonists, or aeronauts as they were called, could reach a height of one thousand feet. This would be a "great vantage for miles around." They used telegraphs or signal flags to communicate with the ground. The brothers were frequently together; as we shall see, Adolfo frequently looked after his older brother.

According to Adolfo, the enemy was advancing toward Washington, and they, along with other regiments, moved to its defense. He wrote, "The Rebels at this time were close to the Capital, only about 7 miles from the Capital." The 23rd encamped on Mr. Henry Queen's farm about five miles north of Washington, D.C. While here, on December 14, 1861, the 23rd received its regimental colors. They were presented to the regiment by the State of Pennsylvania. There was a celebration, and Adolfo recorded a large amount of beer and whiskey. Perhaps just as important, "Mother and Mr. Dutton came down today as a visit to Fred and myself—They stop at Mr. Queen's House." He also noted the very severe cold weather that day. Almost two weeks later, it was Christmas, and their mother remained at Queen's home. The brothers ate "our Christmas dinner with mother at Queen's House."

The 23rd would remain to defend Washington, D.C., until March 1862. The men did not remain the entire time at Queen's farm. On February 8, 1862, they changed camps to "a new place two miles back on Mr. Clark's Farm." Their colonel was promoted to brigadier general during this time, and Captain Thomas H. Neill became their new regimental colonel. From the time the 23rd was mustered on August 31, it would see plenty of action in the Peninsula Campaign, where the men marched to Alexandria and made their way to the Virginia Peninsula by steamer. By April 4, they were on the Warwick River, and according to Adolfo, the regiment suffered its first casualty. The same week, they participated in the Siege of Yorktown and the Battle of Williamsburg, and from the last week in May 1862 to the first week in June, they were at the Battle of Fair Oaks, also called the Battle of Seven Pines. During this time, Fred fell ill. He could not command Company K, so he could not go out on picket duty. His brother took Fred's company out to do picket duty, where, for the next twenty-four hours, he was engaged with the enemy. Both brothers left the 23rd around the same time. On July 15, 1862, Adolfo was detached and became part of General Humphreys's staff until the war's end. Fred returned to

Philadelphia, where he resigned from the 23rd on July 20, 1862. He signed on for three years with the 114th Pennsylvania Infantry, known as Collis' Zouaves. Field officers included Colonel H.T. Collis, Lieutenant Colonel Frederick F. Cavada and Major Joseph S. Chandler.

Samuel Bates, in his history of the Pennsylvania regiments during the Civil War, wrote, "On the 17th of August, 1861, a company recruited in the city of Philadelphia, known as the Zouaves D' Afrique, under the direction of Charles H.T. Collis, who had served in the Eighteenth Regiment for the Three Months' Campaign, was mustered into the United States Service." It was commanded by Charles H.T. Collis, who had served in the 18th Regiment for three months. After it was mustered, it was to be sent to Fort Slocum, "in the defences [sic] north of the Capital, and shortly afterward, moved to join the army, then resting in Maryland." According to the *Memoirs of Alexander Wallace Givin of the 114th Company F*, the men arrived in Maryland in drenching rain. They were quartered in a storehouse. After having breakfast, they boarded railroad cars and were soon on their way to Washington, D.C. They eventually were sent to the Battle of Antietam. However, they did not participate in the battle, being held in reserve. Sergeant Givin wrote, "As the troops passed us going into battle we cheered them all we could." The 114th would become part of the Army of the Potomac and would finally see action in December 1862 in Fredericksburg.

On November 5, 1862, President Lincoln relieved Major General George B. McClellan of command of the Army of the Potomac. Lincoln wanted a more aggressive general to execute the war. This, he felt, was especially true after the Battle of Antietam. McClellan was replaced with Major General Ambrose Burnside. General Burnside wasted no time. President Lincoln hoped that his new commander would be able to secure a large victory over the Confederates because on January 1, 1863, the Emancipation Proclamation would go into effect. A significant victory by the Union would give him a political win. Major General Burnside wanted to move the army from Falmouth in Virginia across the Rappahannock River to Fredericksburg on the other side. He hoped to surprise the small Confederate army protecting Fredericksburg and use it as a gateway to Richmond, Virginia, the Confederate capital.

Burnside arrived in Falmouth, Virginia, by November 19. The brothers were briefly reunited on the same date. Adolfo was located at Stafford Court House. On November 21, Adolfo was permitted to see his brother. He stayed overnight with his brother—where the two brothers stayed is not recorded. By December 2, 1862, he wrote, they "broke camp and marched to within 2 1/2 miles of Bell Plain landing." There was a heavy snowstorm when they arrived at the landing. On December 10, Adolfo reported to General Humphreys at the Phillip House, where General Burnside had his headquarters, because there was talk that the army was getting ready to move.

A problem that Burnside realized was that all the bridges across the Rappahannock had been destroyed. Anticipating this, he hoped that pontoon boats would be there when he arrived with an army of 100,000. The pontoons were late, caused in part by the heavy snow. Burnside's element of surprise would be lost, given the time it took for the pontoons to arrive and put them in place. Robert E. Lee was able to entrench his more than 75,000 troops on the Sunken Road, also known as Telegraph Road, as well as on Marye's Heights. The heights held a commanding view of Fredericksburg from the south. Lieutenant General James Longstreet and Lieutenant General Thomas "Stonewall" Jackson also formed a line just outside Fredericksburg. They had been able to supply themselves amply and brought up large ordnance that could sweep the entire area below them. The Army of Northern Virginia stretched along a seven-mile line. Longstreet was on the "left along Marye's Heights, west of town. Jackson occupied the heights south of Fredericksburg to the south end of Prospect Hill."

The troops started to assemble the pontoons on December 11, 1862. Barksdale's Mississippians made life for the engineers horrible. They easily picked off the engineers and soldiers working on assembling the pontoons. Burnside ordered that the city be shelled, but the snipers were able to hide from the shelling. Once the bombardment stopped, they resumed their harassment. Union soldiers floated across the river and, in house-to-house combat, forced the snipers to retreat.

Confederate lines that Union troops would eventually encounter were concave in shape, to use the words of American Battlefield Trust. The center where Lee occupied was away from the river. If Burnside sent all his troops toward the center, a crossfire from the left and right would decimate his troops. He decided that he would strike both Longstreet and Jackson's troops. Most of his troops would be directed at Jackson, located on Prospect Hill. He planned to keep Longstreet occupied. Major General George Gordon Meade launched the main attack with the Pennsylvania Reserves. Brigadier General John Gibbon's Division would support Meade.

Union batteries opened up at about 10:00 a.m. and bombarded Jackson for an hour. There was no response from the Confederate gunners. Meade and Gibbon started marching at noon. When they got close to Prospect Hill, Jackson's gunners opened up, forcing Union soldiers to take shelter. The Union began shelling again for roughly an hour, allowing Meade and Gibbon to advance again. A hole was found in Jackson's line in a swampy wooded area that the Confederates thought that Union soldiers could not make their way through. Major General Meade and his Pennsylvanians poured in but could not hold their advance without reinforcement. According to Haggerty, to Meade's right "was another Union brigade, commanded by Brigadier General John Gibbon." They, too, had broken through Confederate defenses.

Fresh Confederate troops started to pour in and forced Meade to fall back. This area was to become known as the "Slaughter Pen" because of the sheer number of Union dead. Meade and Gibbon hoped for relief to keep the gains they made against Jackson's line, but Brigadier General Birney's Divisions did not arrive in time, so they continued to push to the front. In addition to numerous regiments, he also deployed batteries to relieve those trying to support Meade and Gibbon. It was hoped that these batteries would plug up the hole that Meade and Gibbon left during their hasty retreat. Haggerty wrote that Birney had also sent for Brigadier General Robinson's Brigade, of which the 114th was a part.

According to an article in the *Philadelphia Inquirer* published on December 15, 1862, during the morning of December 12, the 114th marched from its camp down near the Rappahannock River and waited there for a few hours. As they waited, the men of the 114th could see the battle going on across the river. They were waiting on "a high hill overlooking the river." When they were given the order to cross at what is known as Franklin's Crossing on the afternoon of the thirteenth, while the men marched down to the crossing located on the river, their band struck up the tune "Hail Columbia." They crossed the pontoon bridge and passed to the left, "where the fight was raging the hardest." According to Frank Rauscher in his book *Music on March*, Lieutenant Colonel Cavada told the regimental band that they were of no service and ordered them to the rear out of danger. They fell back to the Bennett House. It was also where the field hospital was set up for the wounded.

Lieutenant Colonel Federico Cavada was with the brigade but not his 114th Zouaves. Instead, Brigadier General John C. Robinson made Cavada the brigade officer of the day when the brigade crossed the river.

He was in charge of the brigade guard. In other words, he was responsible for maintaining discipline and keeping troops in line when marching. Lieutenant Colonel Cavada was unhappy and did not want to be in the rear of any potential battle. Haggerty wrote that Cavada was quite upset and began telling anyone who would listen that he was dissatisfied and wanted to be in the heat of the battle. General Robinson ordered Cavada to remain where he was placed with the caveat that if the brigade came under attack, he could "turn his command over to a subordinate officer to join his regiment."

When they made it to the front, there was nothing but dust, cannonballs kicking up the soil and "dead and wounded men and horses." They were hurrying to the defense of Randolph and Livingston Batteries and reached them just in time. According to Givin, "As we reached the top of the hill, our troops were being driven back by the enemy. We halted, unslung knapsacks, and formed battlefront and then forward double quick…and charged the enemy, driving them back, capturing hundreds of them and recapturing our own Randolph's Battery." Before this, the 114th briefly faltered as it witnessed the carnage of the Slaughter Pen. Seeing the desperate situation, Colonel Collis saved the day by seizing the national flag from the standard bearer and rallying his men. The 114th saved the battery from being captured, driving the Confederates back to the woods. Givin wrote that after firing a few more rounds from the cannons, "The order was given to up and at them: the battery ceased firing, and we charged past and down to the brow of a hill."

When the 114th approached the woods, the Confederate troops opened up on the advancing soldiers. Generals Birney and Robinson rode down to the 114th. They ordered Colonel Collis to "throw out a line of skirmishers to a ditch about one hundred yards on our side of the woods, occupied by Rebel sharpshooters, who were keeping up a continuous fire upon us." Company F of the 114th was tasked to set up the skirmishing line. According to Givin, he remembered that Collis put his hand on his shoulder and pointed to many trees. He told Givin that they were the objective and that when he reached that point, he should drop. According to Haggerty, the 114th remained on the battlefield from Saturday "until about 7 A.M. on the following Monday." Eventually, the 114th was forced to retreat across the river the night of December 15 to their old camp, recrossing the river at Franklin's Crossing.

While Burnside launched attacks against Jackson, he hoped to divert Longstreet's attention by launching simultaneous attacks against what was called Marye's Heights. This attack occurred on December 13, 1862.

Major General Edwin Sumner ordered the first attack, and like with the attack on Prospect Hill, the soldiers attacking this heavily fortified place would need to cross about half a mile of open ground. Soldiers launched the first attack at noon. They had to traverse a millrace used to run a mill. It was designed to hold water, so it was as deep as a man and double that in width. It was filled with water at the time of the first attack. Waiting for the attackers was a thick stone wall that Longstreet's troops rested behind, complete with artillery above the men at the stone wall. It was a suicide mission. Attack after attack was launched until it was dark. Each Union attack was cut down by gunfire and artillery from behind the wall that lined the Sunken Road below the heights. One Confederate boasted, "A chicken could not live on that field when we open on it." According to the National Park Service, the Army of the Potomac lost three thousand men in about an hour. No soldier would ever get more than twenty-five yards from the stone wall. The Rebels stood behind the stone wall four rows deep; they maintained an almost machine gun fire on the Union troops. Humphrey's attack on Marye's Heights also came on December 13. Adolfo was sent across the river to "reconnoiter the position our Division [*sic*] is to occupy in the town." He returned to the Phillips House to report to General Humphreys. Finally, at 3:00 p.m., they crossed through a bridge near the Lacy House, also known as the Chatham House. It was their turn to try to dislodge the Confederates along the Sunken Road, where the stone wall ran parallel.

According to the National Park Service, "Throughout the early afternoon, General Edwin Sumner had thrown the divisions of French, Hancock, Howard, Griffin, and Whipple against the Confederate line without success. Around mid-afternoon, Burnside ordered the heights to be attacked yet again, this time by the men of General Joseph Hooker's Center Grand Division." This meant that Humphreys's soldiers were to be the next attack. The attack almost did not happen. General Joseph Hooker, who was part of the attack, left the looming assault to talk over the potential loss of life with Burnside, who was across the river. According to the National Park Service, it was falsely thought that the Confederates were starting to leave the heights with their artillery. Instead, they were moving it. Humphreys was ordered to attack at once.

Humphreys's Division endured "shell & solid shot raking the streets in all directions." As they left the town, the Rebel batteries opened up, and General Hooker ordered Humphreys to carry the Sunken Road by bayonet. Adolfo, the staff and Humphreys were at the front leading the charge. A horrible fire was unleashed on them. "Our men fall by hundreds but still keep on. All the staff dismounted, having their horses killed—wounded." Humphreys had two horses shot out from under him and was slightly wounded. The general wrote a report about his attack on Longstreet's position. He had about 4,500 soldiers; they were massed around the Philips House. They received orders at 2:30 p.m. to cross the Rappahannock and enter Fredericksburg. His attack would be the last major assault on the Sunken Road, behind the stone wall on Marye's Heights. Humphreys formed a line for battle on the western side of the millrace. It was felt that the Confederate position could not be taken. When the soldiers crossed the open field, they were blasted apart. Determined, the troops reached within "100 yards of the stone wall at the expense of a 25% causality rate, including 5 of his 7 aides." Adolfo was stunned to believe that anyone could have survived, let alone him, and not be hurt. Adolfo recorded in his diary that "men fell by the hundreds" as they tried to reach the stone wall. December 15 marked defeat for the Army of Potomac. Adolfo returned with the rest of the troops to Falmouth with his division. It was during this time that he inquired about his brother. He was told that his brother had been slightly wounded and that he was in the hospital. In his diary, about the defeat, he wrote, "Poor Burnsides [*sic*]."

January 12, 1863, started one of the most painful episodes of Federico Cavada's life, one that would hound him for the remainder of his life. The regiment commander, Collis, brought charges against Cavada in a court-martial. Collis's first charge was "misbehavior before the enemy." Plainly stated, it was charged that Federico "did behave himself in a cowardly manner in the presence of the enemy." The colonel's second charge was that Cavada was absent without leave. Lieutenant Colonel Cavada pleaded not guilty to both charges. Collis believed that Cavada evaded his responsibility when the chance came to join his regiment. Depending on the testimony, it was reported in the charges that Cavada seemed content in the rear, even going as far as hiding in some bushes. The charges also alleged that he feigned being wounded. Still others testified that he had fallen off his horse, and in his defense, he later claimed that he did not realize the extent of his wounds. He did attempt to go to a regimental hospital because of the pain in his leg. Using Cavada's testimony, Haggerty wrote that Cavada said he had been "present on the field when his regiment was engaged and that he did not leave until after dark." He reiterated that he was thrown from his horse and did not realize the extent of his injuries. It was only when the pain was too much that he sought to go to the hospital. He addressed the charge about being absent from battle by saying that he did attempt to find his regiment, but during the chaos of battle, being in the rear made it difficult.

When the verdict was read, he was found guilty of the first charge but not the second charge. It was ordered that Lieutenant Colonel Cavada forfeit all pay and be "cashiered" or dishonorably discharged. Based on his record and behavior, on May 20, 1863, Abraham Lincoln remitted the charges against Cavada. This episode would resurface at inopportune times during his life, with Collis usually at the bottom of it.

Meanwhile, after Fredericksburg, Burnside would not accept his defeat. He started to draw up new plans for another assault on Fredericksburg. According to Dr. Antonio Rafael de la Cova, who spent much time researching and studying the brothers, Burnside "planned to attack the Confederates from their rear by marching his army several miles beyond Fredericksburg and crossing the Rappahannock River at Banks Ford. When the march started, a rainstorm began that lasted two days. The roads turned to liquid mud, bogging down hundreds of horses, mules, wagon trains, and artillery. Burnside canceled his plans and retreated to their former camp at Stafford Heights opposite Fredericksburg." The Mud March lasted from January 20 to January 23, 1863. Burnside was relieved of command on the twenty-fifth and was replaced by Major General Joseph Hooker. Fred was lucky not to be a part of this next campaign, as he was sick (with what is not stated). On January 18, he went to stay with his brother; while plans were being drawn up for the next attack, he "took Fred in [an] ambulance to his Regiment & brought him back to our camp." The next day, he recieved word: "Orders to move are 12:00 o'clock P.M." Worried about his brother, Adolfo went to Brigadier General Birney to secure Fred being placed on sick leave. It was determined that he could be better cared for at home. Fred was sent home to Philadelphia with another soldier called Casey to care for him while they journeyed back to Philadelphia.

After Fredericksburg, Lincoln appointed Major General Joseph "Fighting Joe" Hooker as commander of the Army of the Potomac. He became the fifth Union general to command the Army of the Potomac. Fredericksburg had been a horrible defeat for the Union. However, Hooker was determined to revitalize the Army of the Potomac and raise morale. It seemed to be working. President Lincoln reviewed the cavalry and the 80,000 soldiers in the first week of April. In his diary, Adolfo wrote that Major General Fogliardi of the Swiss army visited the encampment. He also boosted the number of men under arms to 134,000. Robert E. Lee, still entrenched in Fredericksburg with Stonewall Jackson, had roughly 60,000 men. He was low on food and sent Lieutenant General James Longstreet to forage for food for the Army of Virginia.

Fighting Joe Hooker decided that he was not going to hurl troops at Lee as General Burnside did in Fredericksburg. Instead, he devised a plan to send Major General George Stoneman with his cavalry to the Confederate rear to cut Lee's supplies and communication. This would force Lee to either retreat or fight Hooker's army in a place of Hooker's choosing. He had to distract Lee and his Army of Virginia. He took about one-third of his infantry under Major General John Sedgwick and his 6th Corps and 1st Corps to cross the Rappahannock River at Fredericksburg. He hoped to convince Lee that this was where the Union army would cross. General Hooker, in turn, would take the majority of his troops upstream and cross the Rappahannock and Rapidan Rivers. This would occur above Lee's position at Kelly's Ford. Humphreys's 3rd Division was part of Major General Meade's 5th Corps. Like the rest of the Army of the Potomac, they received their marching order on the morning of April 26, 1863. They departed, said Adolfo, by 2:00 p.m. on August 27, using the same roads they had used earlier in the year during the ill-fated Mud March. Adolfo believed that they marched about eight miles and camped at Hartwood Church, only to resume the march again early in the morning, reaching Kelly's Ford, where again they camped.

By May 1, 1863, Hooker continued moving east from Chancellorsville to Lee's flank, moving along the Orange Turnpike and Orange Plank Road. However, Hooker did not expect that Lee would divide his forces. He sent a force to meet Sedgwick at the crossing before Fredericksburg. Sedgwick had some forty thousand troops facing Lieutenant General Jubal Early's twelve thousand Confederate soldiers. Lee and Stonewall Jackson moved west to stop Hooker. Jackson's Corps along with Lee collided with Hooker's troops at about noon on May 1. This occurred a few miles east of Chancellorsville. Hooker ordered his army to fall back to entrenchments near the crossroads, where the Chancellor's house stood. Instead of attacking the Confederates, he hoped that they would attack his fortified troops. Instead, it was discovered that the Union right flank was pretty much unguarded. This was the 11th Corps, commanded by Major General Oliver Otis Howard. Jackson could use a path no larger than a deer run without being detected. Lee had split his army again by sending Jackson on a twelve-mile journey across the Union front. Lee had a small force holding off Hooker. He would need to reunite with Jackson quickly.

The division reached Chancellorsville at seven o'clock in the morning on May 1. Cavada wrote, "All about here is a dense forest intersected by country roads." This area was a thickly wooded area with dense thickets. The locals called this area the Wilderness. Cavada and Humphreys would make some lower rooms their command center in the house. Adolfo's brother's 3rd Corps was also gathered at the house. There is no indication that the two saw or sought each other out. The soldiers at the Chancellor's house were given orders around noon to move east from Chancellorsville toward Lee's flank, along the Orange Plank Road and Turnpike. Lee would respond by splitting his force to meet the Union at Fredericksburg, while Lee, with Jackson, marched west to meet Hooker. The armies collided about two miles east of Chancellorsville.

During the battle, Hooker seemed to lose his nerve and ordered his army back to the trenches they had constructed near the crossroads. Once again, he decided that instead of going on the offensive, he would have the Rebels attack them. The Union had the advantage of seventy-two thousand soldiers to the attacking Confederate force of forty-five thousand. During the battle, Jackson realized that the Union's right flank, three miles west of Chancellorsville, was unprotected again. Stonewall Jackson took about two-thirds of the Confederate army and marched about twelve miles across the Union front to strike the Union right. Lee was now holding off Hooker with about fourteen thousand soldiers.

On May 2, 1863, Jackson started to attack the Union's right flank, guarded by the 11th Corps. The 114th Pennsylvania was moved on May 2, 1863, according to Samuel P. Bates's *History of the Pennsylvania Volunteers*, "to the center of the line, and with the division made a demonstration upon hearing forces of the enemy moving in the direction of Gordonsville." They came up against Jackson's troops. They drove the enemy off, which enabled some of the men to have a cup of coffee and the first meal they had in more than twenty-four hours. Givin remembered in his diary that the order came to move forward "at double-quick time." They were making good time on the enemy when, he said, "Our Eleventh Corps broke and let the enemy in. Our Brigade was cut off from our Third Corps; this was late on Saturday night." They would take a stand at the Chancellor's house. During the battle, due to exhaustion, Colonel Collis was taken from the field. By Sunday morning, the 114th and other Union troops were falling back as the enemy attacked on both sides of the 114th. By May 3, Lee was able to reunite with Jackson. After Jackson was wounded by friendly fire, J.E.B. Stuart took control of Jackson's Corps. Because the Union left an area known as Hazel Grove undefended, the Confederates were able to bring a large amount of artillery up there, which gave the Rebels a clear range over the Union troops. After some five hours of fighting in the woods, the Union started to fall back, encouraging the Confederates to emerge and attack.

Attention now turned to Sedgwick, who was able to break through the Confederate lines at Fredericksburg. He turned west toward Lee's flank. Lee turned and confronted Sedgwick's men after again dividing his men. With just twenty thousand men at Salem Church on May 4, Lee stopped the Union advance, forcing them back across the Rappahannock River. On May 6, the Army of Potomac retreated across the Rappahannock. Again, Givin recorded, "We were ordered to fall back and do it quickly to hold our tin cups so as not to make any noise." They were to cross the Rappahannock River. However, the heavy rains—combined with troops, wagons and horses—created a knee-deep mud march. It made marching very difficult, to say the least. The 114th finally came in sight of the pontoon bridges, and the men were able to get across the river. They crossed the river May 5–6, 1863. "It was a sad day for us, for we left many of our brave comrades either dead or dying, wounded or prisoner in the hands of the enemy." When word of the defeat reached Lincoln, the president responded, "My God— What will the country say." This defeat laid the groundwork for Lee to move his army north to a town called Gettysburg. On May 7, in camp, Adolfo reflected on the defeat at Chancellorsville: "Another grand movement, another terrible bloody battle fought by the Army of the Potomac resulting in so many killed, so many wounded, so many prisoners…and we retraced our steps to our old camps to mourn the loss of thousands of our brave men uselessly slaughtered." He noted, "Burnsides' 'Magnificent folly' & Hooker's 'Magnificent blunder' now stand side by side."

The 114th also went back to camp. Givin wrote that while in camp, Colonel Collis was arrested and charged with cowardice during the battle. At this point, Cavada was made commander of the 114th Regiment. The order came from regimental headquarters. Cavada also made Givin a sergeant major. Collis was wounded during the battle, and he also contracted typhoid. Some believe it might have been malaria. It is important to point out that Collis would be exonerated on the charges of cowardice. His ill health kept him out of the fighting at Gettysburg, which meant a greater role for Lieutenant Colonel Frederick Cavada.

After the battle, Cavada was cited in the report written by Colonel Charles H.T. Collis from his sick bed. This was from the same man who was so hyper-critical of his second in command earlier. "I am happy to testify to the good conduct of Lieutenant Colonel Cavada during Friday and Saturday. On Sunday, during the engagement, he was not with the regiment but informs me that, having lost the regiment, he reported to General Greene, who placed him in command of the One Hundred and Ninth Pennsylvania Volunteers, which regiment he led into action. He reported to me at 12 o'clock, restored to duty by order of General Birney, he having been previously under arrest."

In the *Official Records of the Confederate and Union Armies*, Captain Edward R. Bowen filed a report on the events of July 1–2 at the Battle of Gettysburg. He wrote his report from Fox's Gap, South Mountain, Maryland, on July 12, 1863. He detailed that the regiment left Emmitsburg, Maryland, around two o'clock in the afternoon, marching toward Gettysburg in what was described as a tough march. Givin believed that the orders were to follow Lee and prevent them "if possible from crossing the Potomac." They reached Gettysburg that evening at about 7:00 p.m. and set up camp for the night "on the south side of town." According to Edward J. Hagerty in his book *Collis' Zouaves*, they camped "that night on Cemetery Ridge."

The following morning, Bates wrote in his *History of the Pennsylvania Volunteers* that the 114th went into position early on the "morning of the 2d, on the slight ridge along which the Emmitsburg Pike runs, with its left resting near Round Top." This would have been near the Weikert Farm. The 1st Brigade, of which the 114th was a part, was now commanded by General Graham. They were "posted at the angle formed by this disposition, and in the most trying and exposed part of the field. The One Hundred and Fourteenth held the centre of the brigade line, resting upon the Emmitsburg Pike, just opposite Joseph Sherfy's House." The 63rd was deployed a short distance in front of skirmishers, and the fire opened at about 9:00 a.m. The rebel skirmishers took cover in the tall grass, forming a line and using a fence for cover.

When they marched into battle, Clark's 1st New Jersey battery "took up a position in front and opened on the enemy." This would have been about 2:00 p.m. Cavada, with the 114th, remained in position until they were ordered to advance with the 57th when they reached an oat field. They continued with the 105th on their right and the 68th on their left. When the Confederate batteries opened up, they were ordered to lie down for protection. Confederate batteries were fired for more than two hours. Artillery began to quiet down around 6:00 p.m. Fearing that his light artillery would fall into the hands of the Confederates, Chief of Artillery Captain George E. Randolph rode up on his horse to the Zouaves and ordered them to advance. According to Bowen's report, he stated, "If you want to save my battery, move forward. I cannot find the general. I give the order on my own responsibility." Cavada and his 114th crossed the road and formed for battle.

The 114th advanced to the rear of "the brick house," which would have been the Sherfy House. According to Hagerty, quoting from a soldier's diary, "Sergeant Givin ran up to the Sherfy building in advance of the regiment and knelt looking out between the house and the barn. Cavada, kneeling next to him, asked if the rebels were coming. 'You bet your life they are.'"

It was observed that the Confederates were advancing in superior numbers. Once at the Sherfy House, Bowen and other officers tried to form a line with the 57th, "who were already there." Bowen's official report

The Peach Orchard. *Library of Congress.*

described the fire as a "murderous fire." The night was coming and, with it, more confusion. The 114th fought mainly around the Sherfy House and barn against General William Barksdale's Mississippi Brigade. Its attempts to hold the land around the Sherfy House failed around 6:00 p.m., and the men were forced to retreat up Emmitsburg Road and head for Cemetery Ridge. During this time, the retreating 114th, along with Bowen and Givin, passed a small home used as a shoemaker's shop. According to Bowen's report, Lieutenant Colonel Cavada was found sitting on the back steps of this structure. He replied that he was not wounded but was too exhausted to move. Bowen and Givin offered to help Cavada, but the lieutenant colonel waved them away. He was taken as a prisoner on July 2, 1863.

On the same day, Frederick's youngest brother was a short distance away from the Sherfy House. According to the National Park Service, the 2nd Division under command of Brigadier General Andrew A. Humphreys was near the Peach Orchard northward along Emmitsburg Road. Adolfo kept a diary during the war. His diary is invaluable. Not only does he discuss Gettysburg, but he also mentions his brother, whom he calls Fred. He wrote, "I saw Graham's Brigade move forward, the 114th P.V. commanded by Fred, and conspicuous in their Zouave uniform, took the lead and reached the road under a heavy fire from the enemy's batteries and sharpshooters." Years later, in the Towanda, Pennsylvania *Bradford Reporter*, on December 14, 1865, Adolfo stated that he rode up to his brother just before he was given the order to move up and shook his brother's hand. He told him goodbye and to look after himself.

Adolfo wrote in his diary, "While standing by Seeley's battery, I looked toward the left to ascertain the condition of things and try to make out the Zouaves, in whom I felt a particular interest at that moment. The enemy's fire slackened for a moment, then came to a rebel 'cheer' sounding like a continuous yelp; nearer and nearer it came, the 'red legs' jumped to their feet, volley rained into them, and another regiment formed alongside it." He continued in his diary explaining how the Red Legs, named such because of the prominent red fabric on the legs of their uniforms, returned fire bravely, but the advancing Rebels were on them too quickly. This was in the general location of the John Sherfy House and barn, where the current monument to the 114th is located. Although the Union batteries did their best, the troops were still pressed back. "The breeze blowing from the southward carried the heavy sulfurous smoke in clouds along the ground, sometimes concealing everything from my view." Adolfo reached Cemetery Ridge, but not before having horses shot out from under him.

Adolfo Fernandez Cavada (*standing at right*). *National Portrait Gallery*.

The night of the battle, Adolfo wrote, "The night was intensely dark; the air laden with mist and pervaded by that strange musty smell peculiar to battlefields immediately after a battle….I need not say what gloomy thoughts filled my mind as I lay on the ground. My brother's fate I knew not yet, and I had every reason to believe that he had fallen in that fearful charge and perhaps lay dead or wounded within the rebel lines or a prisoner in their hands."

By July 4, Adolfo still had no idea what had become of his brother. He wrote again, "I rode out to the front and over a portion of the field in hopes of getting some tidings, some clue to Fred's condition. Capt. Bowen of the 114th Regt. Commanding the regiment since Fred's disappearance informed me that he had seen him trying to get off the field when the regiment was surrounded. That Fred had fallen or been knocked down and that he was much exhausted and unable to proceed farther. Some of the men of the regiment had seen him fall. Others knew that he was captured, having seen the rebs envelop him while trying to form some of his men, but the general deduction was that he was wounded and a prisoner."

Givin also recorded the period before Cavada was captured. He wrote that the 114th met the Rebels at the Sherfy House: "The rebels advanced in two lines and in good order until they reached the barn, when our boys met them. Then began a desperate conflict, men on both armies clubbing each other with their muskets." The enemy eventually gained control of the Emmitsburg Road. They drove the 114th back and brought up "a battery of 12 pounders, planting it in the middle of the road opened up with double grape and canister." The 114th began to retreat slowly while the men loaded and fired at the enemy. He remembered they crossed a road, and a small frame dwelling there was used as a shoe repair shop. Lieutenant Colonel Cavada was sitting on the back steps. Givin was with Bowen and inquired if the lieutenant colonel was wounded, and he answered no, saying that he was just exhausted and could not go on anymore. When Bowen and Givin wanted to help him, he waved them away and told them to save themselves. What remained of the 114th made its way to the Baltimore Pike. It was dark by then. After realizing that Cavada had been captured, Bowen decided to command the 114th. The retreating soldiers spent the night in a field alongside the Baltimore Pike.

Joseph Sherfy House, 1946. *Library of Congress.*

"A Future Brigadier." *From* Libby Life *by Fred Cavada.*

Lieutenant Colonel Cavada was sent to an officers' prison along with Brigade Commander Charles K. Graham. The camp was called Libby Prison and was located in Richmond, Virginia. The *Philadelphia Inquirer* on July 8, 1863, carried news of Frederick's capture. During his time there, Frederick Cavada started a memoir of his time as a prisoner of war. He opened the memoir: "Early in the morning of 3 July 1863, a long, straggling column of federal prisoners, captured during the proceeding day on the battlefield of Gettysburg, was marching on the Chambersburg Road to the rear of the rebel lines." He recalled seeing General Robert E. Lee. They were allowed to rest by Willoughby Creek in the woods about three miles from the front.

On July 4, 1863, after the Rebels were defeated, they were to march again in "torrents of rain which fell without intermission." He estimated that about two thousand prisoners were with him. By midnight, they reached "Monterey Springs." Finally, they were able to eat on the morning of July 5. It did not last long because Union troops pursued the Confederates, forcing them to march again. Late in the evening, they passed through Waynesboro and marched all night. They were allowed to rest for one hour on July 6, at 9:00 a.m., when they reached Hagerstown, Maryland. On July 8, they used a rope ferry to cross the Potomac.

At Libby Prison, boredom was always present. Cavada wrote and drew about life in the officers' camp to alleviate boredom. In his book about Cavada written in 1871, O.W. Davis describes that his friend wrote "upon the margins of a newspaper and such other scraps of paper." It took some time before word made it back to Philadelphia, probably by way of Adolfo, that Fred had been captured. Their mother, Mrs. Samuel Dutton, immediately wanted to head to Virginia to see her son. On March 7, 1864, a pass was requested for her "to Ft. Monroe. This lady has a son in Libby Prison, Lt. Col. F.F. Cavada." She also wished to see General Butler because she had a letter from Pennsylvania Governor Andrew Curtain. Dutton had still not seen her son by October 1864.

The year prior was an election year in Pennsylvania. To make life a little bit more normal, the *Chicago Tribune* reported on October 30, 1863, that the prisoners from Pennsylvania held an election for governor and other state offices. The winner was A.G. Curtin. One of the inspectors who ensured that the election was carried out properly was Cavada, appointed by fellow Pennsylvania prisoners.

Mrs. Dutton continued to try to see her son. Robert E. Peterson, in a letter to President Lincoln, wrote that Mrs. Cavada was a very old lady and the mother of Lieutenant Colonel Cavada. His mother had even personally visited the War Department to push her request. Peterson related that she was treated badly by the Secretary of War Stanton. "She was so insulted that she says she wished to have been a man to have knocked him down." It appears that before she could see her son, he was paroled with other officers in January 1864. The memoir Federico constructed during his time at Libby was smuggled out. His fellow prisoners helped Cavada hide the pieces of his manuscript wherever they could find space.

Cavada returned to his family in Philadelphia. He was quite underweight, and his health had suffered being in prison. If he hoped for rest and time to recuperate, it was not to be. The colonel of the 114th Regiment once again leveled charges against his junior officer, accusing Cavada of purposely allowing himself to be captured. Incensed at the accusation by a man who was not even in the battle, Federico Cavada challenged Collis to a duel, which was against military and state law. When General George Cadwalader, commander of Philadelphia, found out about the proposed duel between the two officers, he stopped it. Since Federico had been the challenger, the general placed Cavada under house arrest as long as he continued to reside in the city. He was housed in the Continental Hotel.

Many who knew Federico could not believe that he had challenged anyone to a duel. They also knew that he was in such poor health that it was extremely unlikely that he could even carry out his threat. Oscar Wilson Davis decided to intervene, convincing Federico to meet with Cadwalader. Davis vouched for his friend's character. Once the general met Federico, he was struck by the appearance of the lieutenant colonel, who was described as emaciated.

Cadwalader released Cavada from house arrest and ordered him to regain his strength. He wanted the lieutenant colonel to rejoin his troops in the field when he was officially exchanged with the Confederacy and not just paroled. The former would happen in March 1864. Cavada told his close friends that his poor health as well as the constant accusations of cowardice were taking a toll on him. He hoped to resign his officer's commission and return to Cuba to regain his health. Once again, he was dissuaded from resigning. Influential friends were able to secure him a position on the staff of General David B. Birney. However, General Birney died in October 1864 from what is believed to have been typhoid fever. After Birney's death, Cavada became determined to return to Cuba. He hoped that he could help the United States while there, maybe in a diplomatic role. O. Wilson Davis decided to help his friend achieve his dream after a chance meeting between the two friends.

Davis recalled in his biography that he saw Cavada shortly after he resigned from the Union army. Davis was on his way to Washington, D.C., and after hearing that Cavada wished to serve the United States in Cuba, Davis told

"Our Mess." *From* Libby Life *by Fred Cavada.*

Collis (*left*) of the 114th Pennsylvania Infantry. *Library of Congress.*

him that he could introduce him to people at the State Department. Davis invited him to Washington. Cavada decided that it would be a good idea and went with Davis. He explained that he did not personally know Secretary of State Seward but did know people who knew him.

Once in Washington, D.C., the two men went to the State Department, where Davis saw his friend Edward S. Sanford. This individual, Seward and Davis's mutual friend, arranged the meeting. It was announced that Cavada would become the next consul for the United States at Trinidad de Cuba. He would hold this position from 1864 to 1869. His youngest brother, who had left the army in 1865, became the U.S. consul to Cienfuegos, Cuba. However, after hearing about Federico Cavada's appointment, Collis fired off a letter to Secretary of State Seward, questioning Cavada's fitness for the appointment. According to Davis, there is no reason to believe that Seward put any faith in the letter but did investigate the issue surrounding it.

Both Cavada brothers resigned as consuls in Cuba in 1869 after serving a few years. Events were rapidly moving forward on the island, which Spain still owned. Cuba was agitating for their independence. The revolution started in 1868 and was led by a sugar planter named Carlos Manuel de Cespedes. He declared Cuba a republic in October 1868. This war would last for ten years but would not achieve the independence from Spain so desperately wanted. Eventually, on January 5, 1869, Federico Cavada became the commander of all the Cuban forces fighting the Spanish. Cavada knew Cespedes's chief of staff, General Thomas Jordan, who had inspired Cavada to leave his position as consul to join the fight.

During his time in the Cuban army, Cavada used a scorched earth policy. He burned Spanish property and sugar fields to destroy their wealth. The Spanish began to refer to him as "General Fire." During the war, he was badly wounded in 1870. This occurred, according to friends who knew him, such as Davis, by way of a gun being used by a soldier. It accidentally discharged, striking the general. He was spirited away to a cave well hidden in the mountains. While there, he penned a poem, "The Cave of Bellamar," published in *Harper's New Monthly Magazine* in November 1870.

On June 30, 1871, Cavada was captured by the Spanish gunboat *Neptuno* while he was trying to leave Cuba. He was taken to Puerto Principe, where the Spanish government had tried him in absentia for crimes. When word came that he had been captured, O. Wilson Davis started to organize well-placed friends, such as those in the administration of President Grant, former generals and other influential people; these were people living in the United States or serving in Spain. One such person was General Sickles, who was minister to Madrid. Davis, in letters, asked them to use their influence to intervene on behalf of Federico Cavada. Davis did not know that, in all likelihood, Cavada was executed by firing squad on July 1, 1871. Reportedly, his last words were, "Adiós Cuba, para siempre" ("Goodbye Cuba, forever"). There is no way of knowing where he is buried. He refused the last rites from a priest just before his execution. Because of this, he was not allowed to be buried in consecrated grounds. His grave was left unmarked.

Roughly half a year later, on December 18, 1871, Adolfo was killed, according to the *Boston Daily Evening Transcript*, at La Adelaida near St. Jago de Cuba. He had been appointed a major general on February 6, 1869, to command Cienfuegos. After his brother died, he was appointed to his brother's position. The newspaper stated that he died of a fever, but most have written that he died during battle, having been shot. Many place his death at the coffee estate in La Adelaida near Santiago de Cuba.

Emilio, the oldest of the three brothers, was the only one left. He passed away in 1914. He carried on the memory of his brothers and lived a long life. He, too, later returned to Cuba during the Cuban Revolution. Emilio served as a doctor in the revolution (1895–98) and later settled in Cuba. Emilio helped his brothers by raising funds for the Cuban rebels and sending arms and other supplies. There were lots of coded letters sent back and forth between the brothers.

PART II

THE CONFEDERACY

Maria Dolores "Lola" Sánchez

olonel Dickison wrote, "I have the honor to report that on the evening of the 23rd instant, while the Steamer Columbine was on her downward trip, I engaged her at Horse Landing with a section of Milton Artillery commanded by Lieutenant Bates, and 20 picked riflemen from my cavalry force." The Confederate officer continued with delight, noting that "after the second fire from our battery she became disabled." Canister, solid shot and sharpshooters continued to take their toll on the Union steamer. The ship became disabled after its rudder was destroyed, and within forty-five minutes a "white flag was hoisted." The Union forces, known as the Southern Blockading Squadron, had been taken by surprise. They were the unknowing recipients of intelligence gathered at the Sánchez house from an unguarded conversation overheard by a Confederate spy, Maria Dolores Sánchez. Many just knew her as "Lola."

During her lifetime, Lola Sánchez lived in relative anonymity. Some knew of her bravery, but only when her story was told to newspaers after the war did Lola become a legend—*Confederate Veterans* called her a "heroine." According to the *Intelligencer* from May 10, 1905, the Sánchez family "lived opposite Palatka, on the east bank of the St. Johns River, Florida." The St. Augustine Historical Society believes that they did not live at Palatka but rather a short distance north of what later became Federal Point on a St. Johns River tributary known as the Moccasin Branch River. A researcher at the society proposed that they were linked to Federal Point, which during this time was known as DuPont Point because it might have been the closest post office, as well as being a short distance from the family.

The family had a long history in the area, harkening back to Mauricio del Carmen "Maurice" Sánchez. Although some sources document him being born in the West Indies, several historians and documents indicate that he was born September 22, 1799, in St. Augustine, Florida, part of Spain. Maurice is sometimes listed as being from Cuba, as Norman K. Brewer Sr. and Ranny Elizabeth Brewer note in their genealogy of the Sánchez family that families "traveled to and from Cuba quite frequently, and this is one of the reasons why some of their children were born in that area." The Battlefield Trust states in an article written by descendant Brad Coker that Jose de Sánchez Ortigosa, Jr., Lola's grandfather, was born in St. Augustine in 1724 and was "among those who fled to Cuba in 1764 when Florida was ceded to Great Britain following the Seven Years' War. He returned to Florida following the British departure after the American Revolution and appeared in the 1793 Spanish census." The Roman Catholic Church of St. Augustine has Mauricio—sometimes recorded as "Maurice" and still other times "Morris"—as being born in Florida. It is important to note that Florida was not part of the United States during this time. East and West Florida became part of the United States in 1821 under the Adam-Onis Treaty of 1821 with Spain. It became a state in 1845.

Maurice married Maria Ysabel Oliveros, born in 1818, on September 23, 1838. According to church records, housed in St. Augustine, Florida, Maurice took an active part in the local militia. He participated in the wars between Florida and Native Americans as a private in Dummett's Company. His compiled military records indicate that he enlisted in St. Augustine in May 1836 with a "sorrel mare." Mauricio enlisted for four months and would enlist again in September 1836 for the duration. We know that the Sánchezes were living in St. Augustine by 1840. Here, the couple had their first child, Manuel Ramon, born in 1839. According to the federal census, two years later, a daughter named Francesca Segunda "Panchita" Sánchez was born, followed two years later by Maria Delores, called "Lola" by the family. Three years later, Eugenia was born in 1847. The couple's last child was Maurice Jr., born in 1848. According to the 1850 census, Maurice was fifty-three and a farmer. He was wealthy, with a personal value of $2,000. In the same census, his wife, Maria, was thirty-one, Francis was eight, Dolores was five, Eugenia was three and Mauricio was the youngest at one. According to the same 1850 census, the Sánchez family owned six enslaved persons aged three to thirty-five. They were listed as four males and two females.

According to the 1860 federal census, Maurice, sometimes called Morris, listed his real estate value at $3,500 and his personal estate at $5,200. Additionally, in 1860, his occupation was recorded as a butcher. Tragedy struck the family in 1860 when Maurice Jr. died. The same year, in the federal census, Maurice was recorded as still owning enslaved persons. The reason for the occupation change is unknown, but his personal wealth had increased to $8,700. In this census, he is recorded as having been born in Florida. The children who lived at home were Dolores, Eugenia, Manuel and Francis. Family and newspaper accounts from later periods record that Maurice and his wife were ill. Their ailments are not revealed, but it is believed that Maria was confined to a wheelchair.

In Florida's Ordinance of Secession, according to the Museum of Florida History, the state left the Union on January 10, 1861, noting, "The State of Florida is hereby declared a Sovereign and Independent Nation." President Lincoln, on April 19, 1861, ordered a blockade of the Southern coastline and ports. Eliot Kleinberg wrote that nearly half of the Confederate coastline was in Florida. However, the state was overlooked in many ways during the Civil War. This is because the 1860 federal census showed a sparsely populated state. Only about 140,000 individuals lived in Florida, and of that number, almost 60,000 were enslaved people. Once Florida joined the Confederate States of America on April 22, 1861, the Union quickly occupied St. Augustine in 1862.

Florida seemed to be the forgotten state in the Confederacy until Mississippi fell under the control of the Union. Florida's military supplies became vital to the war effort. This was especially true when Texas's beef was cut off from the Eastern Confederacy. Florida's beef became essential to feeding Confederate troops. Most of the major towns and ports were controlled by the Union. However, as much as the Union tried to penetrate the interior, it could not bring it under control. The most important waterway to transport supplies to Confederate troops became the St. Johns River and its tributaries.

The St. Johns is the longest river in Florida at 310 miles. According to the National Archives, it is also one of only three rivers in the United States that flows north. It begins south of today's Cape Canaveral and "ends up as one of the largest deep-water ports on the Atlantic at its mouth in Jacksonville." Because the river became essential to the Confederacy during the Civil War, it also became essential for Union gunboats to control the river and stop blockade runners from utilizing the interior.

By 1862, the Union army was occupying the area surrounding the Sánchez's home. Union gunboats heavily patrolled the St. Johns. Daniel L. Schafer, author of *Thunder on the River*, wrote that the Union navy continued "to dominate the St. Johns, but skillful application of underwater explosives—called torpedo mines at the time—almost succeeded in closing the St. Johns to federal gunboats." Excursions by Union gunboats continued into 1863. This was the year that the Sánchez family would be directly affected.

Writing from near Palatka on April 2, 1863, Thomas T. Russell wrote to Brigadier General Joseph Finegan describing that on March 23, 1863, "a large sidewheel steamer came up the river as far as Palatka and fired four shells over the town." After this shelling, Thomas T. Russell wrote to Brigadier General Joseph Finegan on April 2, 1863, "They returned to Orange mill." On March 27, 1863, "a large propeller" went up the river and "lay off the mill until evening, when she came up opposite Palatka, abreast of the residence of Mr. Antonio Baza." He continued, noting that "a large force of African-American soldiers landed from the propeller at the residence of Mr. C. Dupont and also at Orange Mill, which said force marched by land to Mr. Baza's and Mr. Sachez's place, opposite Palatka, where they joined the force on board the propeller." They arrived at the residences of Messrs. Sánchez and Baza, surrounded the places, "and took 3 Negroes from Mr. Morris Sánchez and other things of value from the yard." William D. Chislom wrote in the *Columbia Star* that "the Yankees knew someone was giving information to the Confederates, but they had thought it was Mr. Sánchez." The soldiers "encamped that night on the banks of the river in Baza's field."

The next day, March 28, 1863, the ships floated over to Palatka and went to the dock. After they landed some men on the shore, Colonel J.J. Dickison and his company opened fire in a surprise attack. The ships were able to make it back to Mr. Baza. He had been taken as a prisoner when the ships made their way back down the river.

On March 23, 1864, Acting Master John C. Champion wrote to the acting commander of the naval forces on the St. Johns River that he proceeded up the river with the USS *Pawnee*'s launch and the USS *Columbine*. He continued, noting that on March 10, 1864, they anchored off Palatka. Shortly after anchoring, army transports started to arrive to occupy the town. Colonel Barton was in command of the troops. The *Columbine* proceeded up the river to Buffalo Bluff. A Union sympathizer, Hampton Daniels, "kindly offered to guide us where a quantity of spirits of turpentine and rosin was hidden." Using a launch, they continued up the Ocklawaha River for about five miles. A short distance away, they captured "13 1/2 barrels spirits of turpentine and 25 barrels rosin." The raiding party continued its work, capturing the CSS *Sumter*. During one of the raids, Champion noted that "3 female and 1 male enslaved persons were captured who belonged to the Sánchez family." Finally, sugar works were destroyed, and the raiding party secured additional supplies for the Confederate army in the East.

Especially after the torpedoes in the river sank more than a few Union vessels, troops stepped up raids, looking for the people responsible for the building and placing of explosive devices along the St. Johns. Once again, according to Schafer, by April 21, 1864, the Union "stepped up surveillance activity along the river and begun raiding homes of known Confederate supporters."

During one of the raids, Maurice was arrested and taken to St. Augustine, where he was placed in the guardhouse. According to the *Department of the South Census, for 1864*, Maurice was confined to the guardhouse and received rations from the Union army. Recorded in the census was a description of Maurice. He was "5'10" with dark eyes and dark hair." He was sixty-five years old. Perhaps in an attempt to secure his freedom, he also took the oath of allegiance to the Union. The reason he was considered a spy might have been because of his son Manuel Ramon, who was a soldier in the Confederate army.

According to his pension from 1907, Manuel enlisted in Jacksonville in May 1861 in Company H of the 2nd Florida Regiment. It was also known as the "St. Augustine Rifles." Captain John Starke enlisted Manuel into the Confederate army. By 1863, Manuel had been seriously wounded in the head during the Battle of Gettysburg on July 2, 1863. The wound happened during the assault on Cemetery Ridge. Manuel was captured and imprisoned at Point Lookout. This prison was located on the Point Lookout Peninsula in the border state of Maryland. Originally a hospital, it was located where the Potomac meets the Chesapeake Bay. Manuel was one of some fifty thousand Confederates who passed through the prison. He was paroled in March 1865.

The National Park Service states that the "conditions for the prisoners severely worsened as the population exploded. The military did not construct barracks or other permanent housing; instead, tents provided inadequate shelter from the sweltering summer heat and brutal winters." The water became contaminated because of inadequate sanitation, and food and other necessities were in short supply. Diseases ran rampant in the prisoner of war camp.

When exactly Lola and her sisters might have become spies can't be ascertained. It might have predated the arrest of her father and the taking of their property. Or perhaps the imprisonment of their brother. Unfortunately, there are no records indicating either way. Some historians have written that many individuals played both sides of the conflict. Union ships did their best to protect those loyal to the Union and root out those who were aiding and abetting the Confederacy. On the surface, the Sánchezes did play up to the Union troops occupying the area around their home.

Where the Sánchez family lived has been referred to as Palatka, but it is believed that they lived on the Moccasin Branch, a river closer to Dupont Point that after 1866 was known as Federal Point. Cornelius Dupont from South Carolina had settled the area. He established a large and rare plantation for the area at Dupont Landing. Dupont mainly grew cotton and citrus, more specifically oranges, which were valuable cash crops. This land, about ten miles northeast of Palatka and Dupont Landing, was even closer.

The deciding moment came in 1864. Union officers ate dinner at the Sánchez home, as they frequently did when occupying the area. It must have added insult to injury. Maybe they were drinking alcohol or just felt they were not being listened to by the family, but they started to let their guard down while talking. They began to discuss plans of the Union navy and a surprise attack on May 21, 1864.

One time, while sitting on the porch, some officers spoke in considerable detail about the Union's plans and strategy for an upcoming attack. Lola overheard the officers discussing the Confederates, who were "higher up on the St. Johns on the west side." The raid would involve the Union gunboat *Columbine*. Lola called her sisters Panchita and Eugenia to her.

The *Columbine* gunboat was an ex-tug built in the 1850s and commissioned by the U.S. Navy in 1862. It was a paddle-wheel steamboat. It had two side wheels and a steam engine. It was part of the South Atlantic Blockade Squadron. The *Columbine* had only been commissioned for about two years when it was pulled from patrolling off Port Royal, South Carolina. It would be deployed to Jacksonville, Florida, patrolling the St. Johns in early March and taking part in an expedition on the St. Johns and the Ocklawaha.

Lola saw her chance to make a small dent in the Union war machine—perhaps a little payback for what she had endured. Her father still languished in the guardhouse, and they were unable to secure his release.

She arranged with her sisters to cover for her while she made her way to Confederate lines to alert them to the Union plans. According to a story recounted in J.L. Underwood's book from 1906, *The Women of the Confederacy*, "stealing softly from the house, she sped to the horse lot and, throwing a saddle on her horse, rode for life to the ferry, a mile distant; there the ferryman took her horse and gave her a boat she rowed herself across the St. Johns," met one Confederate picket, who knew her and gave her his horse. The rider went to Camp Davis and asked to meet with Colonel John Jackson Dickison.

Colonel Dickison, nicknamed the "Swamp Fox," was the commander of the 2nd Florida Cavalry, Company H. It was a small number of about two hundred individuals at full strength. They mostly used guerrilla tactics to harass the Union on the St. Johns. According to the National Park Service, Dickison "controlled almost all of the central portion of the state." His raids were audacious, striking from Gainesville to the outskirts of St. Augustine. "Confederate daring, however, could not hold off indefinitely the immense power of the Federal forces."

The colonel met with Lola Sánchez. She explained to the Confederate officer that on Sunday, the Yankees planned on ascending St. Johns to trap the Confederates. They would also be sending out foraging parties. After explaining the whole situation, the captain took the picket's horse and exited the camp back to the ferry. She left the horse that the Confederate picket had loaned her. Once across the river, she mounted her own horse. Lola arrived back home just in time, not to be missed. Her sisters had done an excellent job covering for her.

Meanwhile, the officers at the Sánchez home had no idea that while they ate, Colonel Dickison left Camp Davis with Confederate soldiers to lay a trap for the unsuspecting Union soldiers. They would cross the St. Johns to the east side to wait. This battle would become known as the Battle of Horse Landing. It would make Lola a hero and the Union's anticipated surprise raid unsuccessful.

In the *Official Records of the Union and Confederate Navies in the War of the Rebellion*, the battle occurred on May 23, 1864. The Confederate's "2nd Florida Cavalry and a battery from the Milton Light Artillery" were able to disable and capture the USS *Columbine*.

Dickison's troops also caught and captured a transport. Many of the Union soldiers were captured or killed. According to some versions of the story, General Chatfield was killed, and Colonel William H. Noble, commander of the 17th Connecticut Infantry, was captured. Noble was eventually paroled in April 1865. It was a humiliating defeat for the Union to lose its gunboat. Rear Admiral John A. Dahlgren summed up the loss: "The loss of the Columbine will be felt most inconveniently; her draft was only 5 or 6 feet, and having only two such steamers, the service of which is needed elsewhere, cannot replace her."

After the Battle of Horse Landing, a "pontoon was captured and renamed 'The Three Sisters'" in honor of these brave young women. The three sisters had one more mission to fulfill. They wanted to have their father released from the St. Augustine jail. He was not a young man; he was in ill health and disabled. Panchita went by herself to St. Augustine after being permitted to travel by a Union officer and was able to secure his release.

Once the war concluded, Lola married Confederate soldier Emanuel Mauricio Lopez, born on September 22, 1842. His enlistment papers described him as having "dark eyes, dark hair, and 5' 7"." Emanuel enlisted in the Confederate army on May 24, 1861. His enlistment place was listed as St. Augustine, Florida, in the 3rd Infantry as a private. His rank would change on March 27, 1863, as he was made a third corporal. Emanuel was wounded on January 3, 1863, at Murfreesboro in Tennessee and in May 1864 at Dallas, Georgia. He was shot through the shoulder, and in Dallas, Georgia, he was shot through the ankle. After the Civil War, he returned to Florida. In 1866, Lola's mother passed away. It is not clear when her father died.

Emanuel's voting rights were restored in 1867. According to their marriage certificate, the couple married on June 1, 1868, in St. Johns, Florida. Two years after their wedding, the 1870 federal census listed the couple as living in St. Augustine, Florida. They were a farming family with a personal estate of $200 and real estate valued at $100. He was listed as a farmer in the 1880 and 1885 federal censuses. They had a large family of eleven children. Lola's sister Eugenia also married a local Confederate soldier, Private Alberto Rogero, a Battle of Horse Landing veteran. Panchita moved from Florida to South Carolina after marrying John R. Miot, a captain in the Confederate army.

Lola died on October 10, 1895, and was buried in the family plot at All Souls Parish Catholic Cemetery in Palatka, Florida. Her husband applied for a pension in 1899, asking for seventy-two dollars per year. This was because of wounds suffered at the Battles of Dallas, Georgia and Murfreesboro. The last we have of Emanuel is the 1900 federal census, although it's possibly a mistake. He is listed as divorced and still a farmer. He passed away in 1907 and was buried in the same cemetery as Lola. Two years later, according to the magazine *Confederate Veterans*, the United Daughters of the Confederacy gathering was held in St. Augustine that year. Lola and her sister's accomplishments for the Confederate war effort were placed on a plaque that would be mounted at the United Daughters of the Confederacy Memorial Buildings in Richmond, Virginia.

Thomas Hernandez

His physical condition is as good as could be expected under the circumstances.
—*Thomas Hernandez's pension*

One of the topics often overlooked in the study of the Civil War is blockade running. Unfortunately, there is not a tremendous amount of information about it because it was illegal. As James Russell Soley wrote in his article "The Blockade Runner," the Confederate government and troops relied on "the bravery of these runners. They were a small group of sailors who sailed goods in and out of Southern seaports under the guns of Northern ships." Thomas L. Hernandez was one of those daring Confederates who risked his life to bring needed supplies to his country.

Before the Civil War started with the firing on Fort Sumter, the South relied on trade with the North. Stephen Wise wrote that it was mostly with New York City. The North was a middleman in the trade with Europe. With the North no longer a partner, the South needed to establish connections with trading houses, primarily with Liverpool in the United Kingdom. In addition, the Confederate government needed ships, which it would also look to Liverpool to furnish. In fact, some of the early blockade runners flew English flags. Thomas Hernandez was one of those early blockade runners.

There is some confusion relating to the exact year Thomas was born or even the day. According to the U.S. census for 1900, Thomas L. Hernandez

Thomas L. Hernandez. *Nancy Pelletier Collection, from* Military Images *magazine.*

was born in November 1823 in Fernandina Beach, Florida. He was the son of Gasper Juan Hernandez and his wife, Margaret Juana Andrew. The couple was married on April 20, 1808, at the Cathedral Parish, St. Augustine, Florida. It has been recorded that their son, Thomas L., was born in 1821; there is at least one exact date of September 25, 1822. By the time Gasper died in 1841, the family had already moved to Savannah, Georgia.

Four years after Gasper died, Thomas L. married Mary Ann Longstead Cazier on October 8, 1845. In the 1850 federal census, Thomas was listed as working in the "water transportation" industry as a pilot. By the time Mary Ann died in 1858, the couple had five children. During this time, it is believed that Hernandez became a pilot on a boat, guiding it through the treacherous sandbars that made travel on the rivers around Georgia precarious. Ten years later, on the eve of the American Civil War, he was still listed as a pilot with five children. A pilot's expertise in waterways was desperately needed.

After the attack on Fort Sumter on April 12, 1861, the Union needed a strategy to defeat the Confederate States of America. It reasoned that the South largely grew cash crops and was agricultural, thus the Southern states were highly dependent on trade with Europe as well as Latin America. General and Chief Winfield Scott, a veteran of the War of 1812 and the Mexican-American War, envisioned a complete blockade of the South, which included its coastline and the Mississippi River. If control of the Mississippi could be obtained, the Confederacy would be split into two. Even prior to Scott, President Abraham Lincoln had already seen this as a logical sequence of events after the Southern states left the Union. Once newspapers heard of the plan, they dubbed it the Anaconda Plan because, like the snake, the plan was to slowly strangle the life out of the South. With three thousand miles of coastline, it was ambitious, considering that the Union did not, on paper, have enough boats. Knowledgeable pilots like Hernandez would be in demand. With an aggressive Union blockade, the South would need fast boats that could run the blockade.

Hernandez was quickly listed as a private; luckily, his compiled military record is still intact. Initially, he was listed in the 1st Georgia Infantry, which had been organized before the war. His enlistment date was August 6, 1861. He was transferred on April 26, 1862, to Company C of the 13th Battalion Infantry. His rank changed to corporal on July 30, 1862, but was later taken down to the rank of private. Why this happened is not exactly clear. He was detached from Company C by Special Order No. 660 and transferred to Company D on December 4, 1862; the 13th Georgia Battery on December

6, 1862; and later, on December 23, 1862, to Company B. During this time, he served in heavy artillery and infantry on the coast of Georgia.

According to Roger Durham in his article on Thomas L. Hernandez in *Military Images*, these special assignments early on in the war utilized Hernandez as a blockade runner as early as November 1861. His first close call came when on November 23, 1861, the *Albion* was "boarded by Lieutenant Wiltse, of the United States navy" from the ship of war *St. Lawrence*. This occurred off the coast of Georgia. He wrote on the register that the ship was not to enter any port of Hampton Roads because of the blockade. His luck ran out later in the month.

He was aboard the runner *Albion* when it attempted to enter Charleston, South Carolina. It was captured by the U.S. gunboat *Penguin*. When he realized the boat was being chased by the *Penguin*, he "veered her course northerly, in the direction of New York." He was sent to New York City as a prisoner, after which he was soon back in action. Once captured, the captain of the ship produced a British registry for Pembroke Saunders, a merchant of Nassau. The cover the boat was using is that it was a British-registered ship going from Nassau to New York.

If we look at the *Official Record of the Union and Confederate Navies*, we can see that Hernandez was asked to pilot the blockade runner *Albion*. On November 26, 1861, Thomas A. Budd, lieutenant commander, reported, "Yesterday captured and sent to New York the schooner Albion, after a chase of one hour." The *Albion* had a British flag flying, but all on board were from Savannah "by their own admission." He continued, "One of the officers, named Hernandez, is said to be a Savannah pilot. The ship and crew were sent to New York City." In *Reports of Cases and Prize*, "The Albion case appears in the Southern District Court of New York before Samuel R. Betts, District Judge of the United States for the Southern District of New York, in January 1862." The *Albion* had "cargo condemned as enemy property, and for a violation of the blockade."

According to the records pertaining to the case, the *Albion* was captured by the USS *Penguin* on November 25, 1861. It had been discovered "making for a port six or seven miles off North Edisto, in South Carolina." Once caught, the captain of the *Albion* showed the ranking officer of the *Penguin* his "certificate of British registry to Pembroke Saunders, of Nassau, N. P." The cargo with a blockade runner was divided up between the U.S. government and those capturing the ship.

Why did these end up in courts when the *Albion* was clearly aiding the Confederate war cause? Before Congress declared war in July 1861,

Abraham Lincoln issued a blockade of all ships, but it was challenged in courts. In this case, it was in New York City.

Later in the year, Thomas was in Halifax, Nova Scotia, where he joined the crew of the brigantine *Standard*. A brigantine is a two-masted sailing ship. The name comes from the type of rigging used on the ship. It was considered a fast ship and easy to maneuver. Its destination was Southern ports. We know about this trip because of a diary kept by James Dixon Jr. from December 16 to December 22, 1861. They reached Halifax aboard the British brigantine *Lilly Dale*.

The *Standard* was loaded with all sorts of dry goods, food and medicine destined for the Confederate government. It eventually outmaneuvered the Union ships enforcing the blockade, which allowed it to drop off its valuable cargo. The *Standard* was eventually sunk. When no longer deemed useful or in danger of being captured, these ships were often times scuttled.

Thomas Hernandez, before he became the pilot of the CSS *Atlanta*, signed on to the runner *Agnes* from Nassau, which was at Darien, Georgia. He was successful in piloting the *Agnes* in and out of the Union blockade, but on July 8, 1862, it "was captured off Hole-in-the-Wall near Nassau." After being sold in Key West, Florida, it was repurposed again as a runner with Hernandez, only to be caught again, according to Dixon, on September 25, 1862, "as she tried to slip into Saint Andrews, Georgia." Ships were in such high demand for the Confederacy that such vessels had many "lives." There were ships that were built or used for one purpose and later used for another purpose.

The following year, Hernandez, according to his compiled military records, was stationed at the Thunderbolt Battery on the coast of Georgia, September 1862–December 1862. In 1863, he was detained again on a special service in Savannah. His next assignment would be aboard the CSS *Atlanta*, again as a blockade runner. He was one of the three pilots on the *Atlanta*. It would be his most harrowing experience to date. Once apprehended, he was sent to a Union prison.

Captain John Rodgers, senior officer present on the USS *Weehawken*, reported on June 18, 1863, that the USS ironclad *Nahant* and the USS *Weehawken* had captured the "rebel ironclad steamer Atlanta." The Union ships first discovered the *Atlanta* early on June 17, 1863, about "3 miles distant" from the Wilmington River and approaching the blockade. They thought it was a usual ship "that had reconnoitered us daily at about this hour, but a few movements sufficed to show us the true character of the vessel." The *Atlanta* fired a shot but did not hit. The *Weehawken* turned

Thomas L. Hernandez (*sitting third from left, with the long beard*), outside prison, Fort Warren, Boston. *Naval History and Heritage Command*.

toward the enemy. By 5:00 a.m., "the Weehawken closed with the enemy and opened fire on him with accuracy." The *Atlanta* hoisted a white flag. The *Atlanta* had run aground and remained helpless.

During an exchange with the *Weehawken*, one of the shells from the Union ship hit the pilothouse, wounding all the pilots, including Hernandez. After hoisting the white flag, the entire crew was captured. Hernandez was sent to a Union hospital in Hilton Head, South Carolina, to recover. Later, the rest of the crew, including Hernandez, were sent to New York City. It was from New York City that they would be heading to Fort Warren, located in Boston Harbor. A photo of Hernandez exists of his time incarcerated in Fort Warren. He was paroled the same year the *Atlanta* was captured. According to his military record, from January to February 1864, Hernandez was "transferred to the C.S. Navy and dropped from the role on February 1, 1864." He was paroled on September 28, 1864, and exchanged on October 18, 1864, at Cox Wharf.

According to Confederate records housed in the National Archives, Hernandez was commissioned a pilot on the CSS *Savannah* on October 27, 1864. The following month, on November 18, 1864, in a reply to Captain S.S. Lee, CSN, who inquired of Flag Officer William W. Hunter what assignments he had for two pilots, one of whom was Thomas. However, for some reason, he erroneously recorded Thomas as Austin Hernandez. There was also another pilot named Fleetwood. It turned out that pilots were in such high demand that they had already reported for duty. His letter concluded with, "I have given no directions in relation to pay for these pilots; they having been already employed in the service, I presumed that their rate of pay had been established." At the end of the month, a pay receipt was sent to Hernandez for $100 per month. The orders were forwarded by Flag Officer William W. Hunter on October 27, 1864. Hunter's order was the following, addressed to "Pilot Thomas L. Hernandez, C.S.N." It read: "You will be pleased to report for duty on board the Confederate steamer Savannah." He was transferred again on December 4, 1864, to the Confederate steamer *Isondiga*. Hernandez replaced a pilot named Austin. On December 20, 1864, Savannah was evacuated; as a direct consequence, Hernandez was sent to the Charleston Navy Yard. This same year, he married his second wife, Jane.

U.S. monitor *Weehawken* and Confederate ram *Atlanta*. *Naval History and Heritage Command.*

In a letter on April 13, 1865, from Augusta, Georgia, Flag Officer Hunter of the Confederate navy notes that in a "Report of Flag-Officer Hunter, C.S. Navy, in response to the Department's order to forward names of unworthy officers holding acting appointments," Hernandez is listed among several names. He does not describe why he feels he is one of a few "unworthy officers holding acting appointments." Although the other officers there are listed with charges against them, none is listed against Hernandez.

Hernandez left the Confederate navy after the war. He returned to Savannah, where he continued to work as a pilot. As noted in the 1870 census, he seemed to have tried his hand as a farmer. He lived with his wife, Jane, and three sons, Edwin, Jasper and William. The following year, he lived at 22 Abber, according to a Savannah directory, and once again was a pilot. In the next decade, he continued as a pilot in Savannah. According to his later testimony in his pension request, it was Savannah Harbor. He later resided at 38 Liberty Street in Savannah.

Sometime around 1890, Hernandez's vision started to decline. The exact ailment is not mentioned. By 1893, he was claiming to be blind in both eyes and, consequently, unable to support himself or his wife. He applied for a pension in 1897 as a Confederate veteran. The U.S. government did not offer pensions to Confederate veterans. It was up to the state governments in the South, which were still rebuilding after the war.

The National Archives in Washington, D.C., records that a state law enacted on December 24, 1887, "permitted financially needy Confederate veterans and widows to apply for a pension." They applied to the state where they lived, not necessarily the state they served in the war. So, in the case of Thomas Hernandez, Georgia started granting pensions in 1870. This pertained to those soldiers with artificial limbs. Almost a decade later, it was expanded to those veterans with other disabilities and to their widows as well if they were indigent. By the time Hernandez applied, it had been expanded again to include "old age and poverty."

Thomas applied for a pension because he was indigent. He listed in his pension application that he had no property or income for the last "several years past he has been supported by contribution." This would have been from family, friends or churches. His doctor wrote that "his physical condition is as good as could be expected under the circumstances." Friends such as Louis Wiggins, whom he had known since 1845, testified on Thomas's behalf. He continued collecting his pension until he died in 1903.

His obituary in the *Savannah Morning News* listed him as the oldest of the Savannah pilots. He died at his home at 405 Joan Street in his eighty-second year. A funeral was held at his residence at 4:00 p.m., attended by members of the Pilot Association. After a service at the Cathedral of St. John the Baptist, he was interred at Laurel Grove Cemetery. In 1910, his widow, Jane, was living on St. Julian Street with one of her children. She is listed in the federal census as a grandmother. She continued to live in Savannah. Jane lived until 1911; she was buried next to him after she passed. The same year, she had applied for a widow's pension. She spent the last year of her life in the Park View Sanatorium.

LORETA JANETA VELÁZQUEZ

There may have been men who did harder fighting at Bull Run than myself, but no one went through the fight with a stouter heart, or with a greater determination to behave valiantly, and, if possible, to give the enemy a sound thrashing.
—*Loreta Janeta Velázquez*

We will not know for sure how many women fought in the American Civil War. This is because these women were not legally fighting in the war. Some even went as far as to dress as men to enter combat or, in some cases, act as spies. Many scholars place the number of women fighting on both sides of the conflict as between 400 and 750, as the American Battlefield Trust believes—a "conservative estimate." This is because of the "inherently clandestine nature of the activity." One of those individuals was Loreta Janeta Velázquez. She fought in combat and also worked as a spy for the Confederacy. Her story is an interesting one, even though most of what we know about her life comes from her autobiography, *The Woman in Battle: A Narrative of Exploits, Adventures, and Travels of Madame Loreta Janeta Velázquez, Otherwise Known as Lieutenant Harry T. Buford, Confederate States Army*. It was written to support her son and was published in 1876.

On June 26, 1842, Loreta Velázquez was born in Havana, Cuba. She was the youngest of six children. Her father was Spanish, and his wife was French American. All she wrote about her mother and father is that her father was "appointed to an official position" in Cuba, which was a part of Spain at that time. While in Cuba, she noted, her father was a diplomat.

Loreta Janeta Velázquez, aka Harry Buford, from her 1876 memoir.

In 1844, her father inherited a large ranch in Mexico. He settled his family in San Luis Potosi. They were not living there long before the Mexican-American War broke out. Mr. Velázquez left to enlist in the Mexican army in order to defeat the Americans. He sent his five children to St. Lucia, which was located in the British West Indies, to stay with his sister's family. By the time the war concluded with the Treaty of Guadalupe Hidalgo, his ranch had been devastated by combat and neglect. Loreta's father gathered up his family and moved back to Cuba, as he had inherited a large plantation at Puerto de Palmas.

As was customary in wealthy families like the Velázquezes, Loreta was educated by a private tutor until 1849. Her father decided to send his youngest child to New Orleans. Loreta's mother had a sister living in New Orleans, and she was placed in charge of Loreta's education. Loreta learned to speak English. She referred to her aunt as "Madame R." While she was pursuing her education, her father decided to arrange a marriage for his fourteen-year-old daughter. Loreta wrote that this was against her wishes. In her autobiography, she referred to the potential suitor as "Raphael R.," a man "I did not feel a particle of affection for." In fact, she had already met someone else, a U.S. Army officer named William Rouch.

Possibly in an effort to derail the marriage, Loreta proclaimed that she was in love with Rouch. In an effort to drive her point home, she openly flirted with Rouch in front of her intended fiancé. William and Loreta exchanged letters and frequently met covertly. In her autobiography, she wrote that with William Rouch, she understood love for the first time. This made her detest Raphael even more than before, and she became determined to discourage him. Continuing to see the flirtation before him, Raphael demanded that Loreta's aunt put a stop to this "affair" happening right before his eyes. Her aunt threatened her that if this did not end, she would be sent back to Cuba, where she would never see this man again.

Loreta did not want to go back to Cuba. She pretended to accept her aunt's decree. Instead, she set up a clandestine meeting with William. It came as a shock when a military officer told her that he was due to be deployed any day. She knew that she needed to act fast because there was a very real chance she would never see him again. This officer told her that it would probably be one of the frontier posts. The couple decided that the best course of action would be to elope. However, before they decided to make their move, one of them suggested that they should try approaching Loreta's father and mother.

The couple was not prepared for the reaction. Her father became enraged after she explained her love for Rouch. He had been vehemently anti-American since the Mexican-American War. He refused to give his approval to his daughter, especially for an American soldier. The couple had no choice but to disobey her father—she decided to elope with Rouch. They were married on April 5, 1856. After the marriage, she returned to her aunt's home, acting as if nothing was wrong. Loreta finally sent Raphael away, explaining to him that she had never loved him. Her aunt threatened to send Loreta back home. Loreta produced her wedding certificate. Once Loreta's father found out what she had done, she was promptly disinherited. Loreta left New Orleans with William, heading west. According to the *Arkansas Encyclopedia*, he was "to participate in army actions against the Mormons in Utah."

Between 1856 and 1860, the couple had three children, all of whom died in infancy. When in April 1861 the Confederates fired on Fort Sumter in Charleston Harbor, setting off the opening of the Civil War, Loreta convinced her husband to join the Confederacy. He acquiesced to his wife's plea and resigned his officer's commission. She claimed that he was awarded a commission in the Confederate army. When he was finally mustered into the army, there was a real threat that the couple would be separated for an extended time. Loreta became distraught about this possibility.

In her autobiography, reflecting on that period, she wrote that her last two children died of fever. About her decision to join her husband in battle, she noted, "My grief at their loss probably had a great influence in reviving my old notions about military glory and of exciting anew my desires to win fame on the battle-field." Earlier in life, she had been captivated by tales of Joan of Arc. Loreta proposed to her husband that she pose as a man and join the army with him. His response was unequivocal, saying that she was to stay home, where a woman belonged. In an effort to convince her not to join the military, while in Memphis, he told her to dress as a man as an experiment. He wanted to show his wife how men could be and just how unsafe her scheme would be. Loreta, donning men's attire, went out for a drink with William. Loreta was undeterred.

Loreta located a tailor to sew her a Confederate uniform. She tried it on and did not feel that it was convincing enough. Loreta found another local tailor to continue to work with her uniform. With the uniform, Loreta also used a false beard and mustache. She adopted the name Harry T. Buford. She wanted to prove to her husband, who was now deployed in Florida, that she could be an effective soldier. Eventually, she traveled to Arkansas, where, according to the *Arkansas Encyclopedia*, she stayed "at the Giles homestead." She wrote that she raised "235 recruits in 4 days." These recruits would become known as the "Arkansas Grays." Loreta intended to deliver the recruits to her husband, who was now in camp at Pensacola, Florida. When she arrived, he thought she was Lieutenant Harry Buford. Once it was safe, she told William who she really was and hoped that he would approve. Loreta had fooled him. Instead of happiness, he reprimanded her as if she were a child. He ordered her to return home. It would be the last time she saw her husband alive.

Dressed again as Buford, she left the camp in Florida for New Orleans. After arriving back in New Orleans, a telegram was waiting for her. She wrote in her autobiography that while "drilling his men, my husband undertook to explain the use of the carbine to one of the sergeants, and the weapon exploded in his hands, killing him almost instantly." She lamented that she was "now alone in the world." She left Lieutenant Thomas DeCaulp in charge of her command and went to look for areas that would see combat. More than ever, she wanted "to take an active part in the war, if only for the purpose of avenging my husband's death." Her first combat test would come at First Bull Run, known to Confederates as First Manassas, on July 21, 1861. When Lieutenant Buford arrived in Virginia, she went toward the Confederate headquarters, where it looked to her the action might be. Buford went around, asking for a command and, at one point, even tried to buy one. She was repeatedly told that there was none to be had. According to the memoir, Brigadier General Milledge Luke Bonham took Buford under his command. It would be her first taste of combat.

During First Bull Run, Buford was at Blackburn's Ford. She wrote that on July 18, "the enemy made a sharp attack." The Union army was repulsed during its initial attack on the Confederates, but the attack grew more determined. An hour later, she remembered, the Confederate army was able to turn back the attack on Blackburn's Ford, which started a Union retreat. It was the beginning of the larger battle of Bull Run. Eager for more action, she was placed in temporary command of a company when the senior officer was killed. As the troops began massing on July 21, 1861, she claimed to have no fear, although it looked like the Confederates would lose the battle. Later in the day, the battle turned in favor of the Confederate army, and it turned into a full rout of the Union army, which retreated to Washington, D.C. Buford wrote, "There may have been men who did harder fighting at Bull Run than myself, but no one went through the fight with a stouter heart, or with a greater determination to behave valiantly, and, if possible, to give the enemy a sound thrashing." On July 18, 1861, there was a burial detail. Buford, along with an enslaved man named Bob, spent a good part of the day burying the Confederate dead.

After the battle, Buford returned to Richmond. As a "freelance soldier," she looked for other places where her services could be useful. If Harry Buford wished for more battles in which she could prove her bravery, they would come. She took part in the Battle of Ball's Bluff in Virginia on October 21, 1861, which was another victory when Confederate troops beat back a Union force. The brutal battle and the carnage took her by surprise. She wrote in 1876, "I did not fully realize the enormities of such a slaughter as was involved in the defeat of the Federals at that place, I have never been able to think of it without a shudder." It affected her enough that she decided to try her hand at becoming a spy.

After the Battle of Ball's Bluff, Lieutenant Harry Buford discarded the alias and became Loreta Velázquez again. This time dressed as a woman, Loreta entered Washington, D.C. While there, she acted as a spy on behalf of the Confederacy to gain intelligence for Jefferson's government. She paid close attention to such things as troop movements, cannon placements and other intelligence. She later claimed that she met President Abraham Lincoln and his secretary of war. Once she gathered enough information, sometimes using the false name Alice Williams, she returned over the Potomac to Richmond, Virginia. In her autobiography, she claims to have been made a detective by General Leonidas Polk. Perhaps being a detective was not to her liking as much as military life. She returned to the army as Lieutenant Harry T. Buford in time for the Battle of Fort Donelson on February 11, 1862, where she remained until the fort fell to Union General Ulysses S. Grant.

Still posing as a Confederate officer, she eventually returned to New Orleans when the city was readying for a Union attack. Suspicion and anxiety were relatively high in the city. When she appeared in the town, Buford was still wearing her uniform, albeit in tatters from battle, hard work and being slept in for days on end. It became apparent to some that she might be a woman. She said, "I was in very low spirits, if not absolutely sick, when I reached New Orleans and was not in a mood to play my part in the best manner." Buford was arrested—at the "Delachaise grounds," according to a local newspaper—for being a spy and was taken before the provost marshal. "I determined that the best, if not the only plan, was to present a bold front and to challenge my accusers to prove anything against me, reserving a revelation of my identity as a last alternative." After the provost marshal questioned her, he decided to let her go. She returned to New Orleans, where she was arrested twice. For the first arrest, she was accused of being a spy again. The second arrest came about from an accusation that she was a woman dressed as a man.

The second charge was considered disorderly conduct. Buford was brought before the mayor of New Orleans. When a Dr. Root from Charity Hospital appeared to question her where she was staying, she knew that he would be hard to dismiss. Buford came clean that she was, in fact, a woman dressed as a soldier. She met with the mayor and asked that she be able to leave the city and never return. He would have nothing of it. Instead, he had her fined ten dollars and confined to jail for ten days. After her time was up, she fled the city to rejoin the army once again as Lieutenant Buford. She eventually joined the Army of East Tennessee. In April 1862, as Buford, she fought in the Battle of Shiloh. This was once again another Confederate defeat. While helping to bury the dead, she was wounded and again returned to New Orleans.

While in New Orleans, this time, Buford became Velázquez again, working as a spy within the city. She was arrested again, but the charges were dropped. Fearing for her life, she fled the city shortly before it fell to Union General Benjamin Butler on May 1, 1862. She eventually arrived in Richmond, only to be arrested there as a spy and placed in Castle Thunder, a Confederate prison. Using her powers of persuasion, she became friends with the commandant, George W. Alexander. Unbelievably, Velázquez was released and once again employed as a spy. She was arrested in Lynchburg, Virginia. Tired of being arrested and possibly fearing for her own personal safety, Velázquez was growing tired of the service. The wound from battle in her foot was becoming more and more painful. She decided to check into a hospital in Atlanta, Georgia.

As Larry Eggleston wrote in *Women in the Civil War*, Lieutenant Thomas DeCaulp kept in touch with Loreta by mail. After her husband's death, his junior officer had confided to his friend's widow that he always harbored strong feelings for her. He had been in love with her back when William was courting her. He just forgot about it because she was already married to his friend. When William died in the accident, he picked up on his feelings for her, writing many letters to her. They unknowingly fought together at Shiloh, where Buford was wounded by a piece of shrapnel, which was why she was in the hospital at the moment. DeCaulp saw Buford as a cherished friend.

In her memoir, she wrote that she wanted to tell him and not have him find out from someone else. While at the hospital, DeCaulp was happy to see Buford. He had come to cherish the young man's friendship. The two men started talking when, according to her memoir, DeCaulp produced a picture of Velázquez. He spoke about how much he missed her and loved her. DeCaulp went on to say that they were to be married after the war. Buford became nervous about revealing herself. If she did, there was the chance that he would reject her. Instead, in a roundabout way, she led him to his discovery. When he realized that the "man" in front of him was none other than his love, he was joyful. The couple decided to take the doctors into their confidence as witnesses so they could be married. The doctors agreed and found a priest who also agreed to the union. They were married.

Velázquez, in her memoirs, wrote, "Our honeymoon was a very brief one. In about a week, he thought himself well enough to report for duty; and he insisted upon going, notwithstanding my entreaties for him to remain until his health was more robust." She returned to civilian life as a woman.

Thomas DeCaulp returned to his command, but on the way, he relapsed with an undisclosed illness. While ill, he was taken prisoner by Union forces and sent to a Union prison in Tennessee, where he died. She was not able to retrieve his body for proper burial. Loreta again wanted to avenge her husband's death. She decided that there was no longer any use in staying out of the war, and she rejoined the Confederate cause.

Eggleston, who drew mainly from her memoirs and newspapers, which are really the only sources of information about Velázquez's life, noted that the first thing she did after shedding her uniform was to pay an African American woman "$20 for a dress, sunbonnet, shawl, and shoes." She disguised herself as a poor woman heading north. Along the way, people took pity on her, giving her better and better clothing as a gift. Loreta wrote that at one point, she was dressed so well that she secured lodgings in the Brown Hotel in Washington, D.C. She soon become a secret agent once again.

After she arrived in D.C., she reported back to Confederate officials on troop movements, defenses and other military intelligence. Eggleston believes that Loreta found out that the Pinkerton Federal Detective Corporation was hiring a detective. She applied using the alias Alice Williams and earned two dollars per day as a "special agent." She successfully joined their ranks, making her a double agent. Her commanding officer at Pinkertons told her to go to Johnson Island Prison in Sandusky Bay, located in Ohio. There was an insurrection brewing in the prison. The detectives wanted information on the people planning the insurrection so they could crush it before it got started. Loreta, using an alias, came through Canada.

In mid-September 1864, Loreta met with Confederate sympathizers in Canada and worked with operatives there in order to help the Confederate cause. She then visited the Johnson Island Prison and helped those individuals who were planning the insurrection. The planned uprising ultimately failed because a prisoner turned informant. What is also of note is that her boss, Lafayette C. Baker, who was the chief detective of the Pinkerton agency in Washington, D.C., felt that something was not quite right about his new hire. He placed another detective on Loreta's trail to find out more about her. He had doubts that she was who she stated she was before taking the job. Before she was made, Loreta left her job with the Pinkerton agency in 1864. She also felt that the job was becoming too dangerous. Perhaps she knew that another detective was on her trail. Loreta still felt determined to help the Confederacy, including traveling to Havana, Cuba, to secure supplies for the Confederacy. Perhaps the most intriguing bit of information uncovered by Blanton and Cook in their book *They Fought Like Demons* was that "in the winter of 1865, while in New York City, she plotted with other Confederate agents to assassinate President Lincoln." Another plot separate from that involving John Wilkes Booth was uncovered by investigators. In a letter in the *Official Records of the Union and Confederate Armies* dated October 10, 1865, and written by Brigadier General Holt, judge advocate general, the plot in question involved the following:

> *The witnesses mentioned by me include all that I have so far obtained, but my investigations have led to the discovery of another plot, approved by Davis, for the murder of the late President quite diabolical as the one which resulted in his death. The witnesses to establish this charge—one of who is a Miss Alice Williams, who was commissioned in the rebel army as a lieutenant under the name Buford.*

After the war ended in April 1865, Loreta married for a third time. She married a former Confederate officer named Major Wasson. In her memoir, she described him as having "long, wavy flaxen hair, which he wore brushed off his forehead, blue eyes, and fair complexion." She still did not give up her dream of the Confederate cause. She started working with the Southern State for the Venezuelan Emigration Company. The newlyweds moved to Caracas, Venezuela, for the purpose of settling former Confederate soldiers. While getting ready to return to the United States, her husband contracted an illness and died. She again returned to the United States, according to a local paper, in January 1867. According to her memoirs, she married again in 1868, when she was living out west in Nevada, to a miner named Edward Hardy Bonner. She went out west for many of the same reasons many other people left the South: better economic opportunity that was not available in the war-torn South. Loreta gave birth to a son, and the family of three relocated to California. While in California, she wrote her memoirs about her time in the Civil War, to be published in 1876.

It is important to point out that not everyone embraced her version of the facts. In two surviving letters from October and November 1876, she addressed one letter to Reverend W. Jones, who reviewed her book. Loreta felt insulted after reading his review of her book in the *Southern Historical Society Papers*. In the letter, she took great pains to point out to Jones that her version of events was her version as she saw them. It was not meant to be a historical account of the war.

Perhaps the most famous person to challenge her version of events was General Jubal Early, a former Confederate officer. Blanton and Cook wrote that Early read the book in 1878 and "concluded that it was false." They continued that "Early was correct in noting chronological inconsistencies" in her book. Early was one of few who questioned its validity. Some historians have pointed out that the book had significant problems and was most likely embellished. In *They Fought Like Demons*, the authors point out that her second husband, Thomas DeCaulp, did not die at the time she noted. He survived the war. He was part of the 3rd Arkansas Cavalry and was reported as a deserter. He later joined the Union army under an alias and married another woman.

Finally, in 2016, William C. Davis published the book *Inventing Loreta Velasquez: Confederate Soldier Impersonator, Media Celebrity, and Con Artist*. Davis maintains that most, if not all, of what Velázquez states is not truthful. He wrote in an article from June 2017 that Velázquez revealed herself to be a prototype of the modern "'media celebrity.' A master at manipulating the press to achieve publicity. Her real name at birth remains unknown." Using newspapers to track her down, Davis came to believe that she might have been a teenage prostitute in New Orleans in 1860, using the name Ann Williams. Like Jubal Early, he sees many inconsistencies in her book and goes as far as to assert that her alleged facts changed throughout her life. Davis also claims that she died much later than 1891. He believes that she died in January 1923 in St. Elizabeth's home for the insane in Washington, D.C. The location of her final resting place remains a mystery. Some still maintain that her story contains truth, and it is a fantastic read for others. There is no doubt that the story of her life will continue to generate controversy for another 140 years.

DAVID CAMDEN DE LEON

*Treason and patriotism are next door neighbors and in accident makes you strike
the right knocker. Revolution is treason even if right, if unsuccessful.*
—*Dr. David Camden de Leon*

The *Boston Daily Globe* stated it best upon the death of Dr.
David Camden de Leon in 1872: "The name will be a strange
one to many who read it, it having found no honorable place
in American history for the last dozen years." Although the name is hardly
recognized today, during Dr. De Leon's lifetime, if you lived in Columbia,
Camden or Charleston, South Carolina, there is no doubt that you would
have been well acquainted with most of his family, or at least his father, who
was mayor or intendent of Columbia, South Carolina, for three terms.

Leonard G. Dauber, writing in the *New York State Journal of Medicine* in
1970, comprehensively researched the De Leon family. He noted that they
were descended from Marrano Jews, originally from León, Spain. The
family fled religious persecution in Europe first by way of Portugal and the
West Indies and then to Savannah, Georgia, by 1733. Abraham de Leon
was the first ancestor to live in the British colonies. According to a genealogy
from 1971 in the South Carolina Historical Society Archives, his son Jacob
relocated to Charleston, South Carolina. Jacob had a son named Abraham
who became a physician. Once again according to Dauber, he graduated
from the University of Pennsylvania Medical School. Abraham was also
"a surgeon's mate during the War of 1812." His other son, and the one we

will follow, was Mordecai Hendricks. Mordecai was a prominent physician in Columbia, South Carolina, and also a mayor or intendent of that city. According to the genealogy housed in the Southern Carolina Archives, he married Rebecca Lopez y Nunez. The couple had a son, David Camden, born on May 6, 1816; a daughter, born in February 1817 but who died in infancy; Edwin, born on May 4, 1818; Agnes, born on April 4, 1819; Maria Louisa, born in 1820; Adeline May, born in 1837; and finally Thomas Cooper, born on May 21, 1839.

There is not much known about David's early life. David pursued an undergraduate degree from South Carolina College, graduating in 1833. After graduating, he decided to take some time off, as was common during that time among the more affluent. David decided to visit Europe. After returning from Europe, David enrolled in the University of Pennsylvania, obtaining his medical degree in 1836. Before joining the U.S. Army, he became a practicing physician in Columbia, South Carolina.

According to Dr. Dauber, De Leon was commissioned an assistant surgeon on August 21, 1838. One of his first deployments would be in Florida. The United States was attempting again to subjugate the Seminoles and remove them west to Indian Territory. This was known as the Second Seminole War. While stationed in Florida, with the 6th Infantry in the field west of the Suwannee River, Dr. De Leon "contracted bilious fever in the autumn of 1840." Florida Memory, which is part of the State Library and Archives of Florida, explains that it was believed during this time that bilious fever was caused by an excess of bile. It is characterized by jaundice, vomiting or "diarrhea containing bile." It is believed that he was suffering from malaria or hepatitis. His illness was serious enough that Dr. De Leon requested sick leave for an extended time until he recovered. After recovering from a bilious fever, Dr. De Leon requested a transfer out of Florida. He cited that the reason was because of the effect the climate had on his health. It was granted, and between June 1842 and August 1845, De Leon was stationed at different times at Fort Pike, Louisiana; Fort Moultrie in Savannah, Georgia; and in Philadelphia. After his service in various locations in the East, De Leon was then stationed on the Gulf of Mexico in Corpus Christi. His first taste of the Southwest would be when he was stationed in 1846 in Santa Fe, New Mexico, during the war with Mexico.

In the 1840s, Manifest Destiny was in full swing in the United States. When Texas was annexed by the United States, it greatly antagonized Mexico. Further complicating the issue was that Mexico claimed that the Texas border with Mexico was at the Nueces River, while the United States maintained that it was the Rio Grande. President Polk meanwhile desired to take control of California and New Mexico Territories. The United States would agree to pay Mexico money if it accepted the Rio Grande as the border, which, of course, it flatly refused. Polk set about to achieve this by force. However, he needed to provoke the Mexican government into acting. This occurred on April 25, 1846, when General Zachary Taylor began patrolling the border on the Rio Grande. Mexican forces attacked the U.S. forces. Congress issued a declaration of war against Mexico on May 13, 1846.

Once the United States declared war on Mexico in 1846, David Camden de Leon was attached to General Zachary Taylor's forces at Matamoras in Mexico. He accompanied Taylor as an assistant surgeon in every battle that involved Taylor, including Vera Cruz. Eventually, for reasons not stated, Dr. De Leon was transferred to Major General Winfield Scott as an assistant

David Camden De Leon.
Jewish Museum of New York.

surgeon in the division commanded by Major General William J. Worth, which was the 1st Division. Dr. De Leon was with General Worth during the Battles of Molino Del Rey on September 8, 1847, and Chapultepec on September 13, 1847. During the battles, numerous officers were wounded or killed. Dr. De Leon, seeing that troops needed guidance, led charges in both battles. This bravery earned him the nickname "the fighting doctor." It is important to point out that many sources, most notably his obituary from 1872, erroneously report that he was thanked for his service and bravery by a Congressional Resolution. According to the U.S. Senate Library, De Leon was not the subject of a Congressional Resolution. His name does appear in President Polk's State of the Union messages that were published as a House of Representatives Document. The attachment in question was penned by Commanding Officer Worth. On September 28, 1846, he wrote, "I have the pleasure to add my personal observation. In common with the entire division, my particular thanks are tendered to Assistant Surgeons Porter (Senior) Byrne, Conrad, De Leon, and Robert (medical department), who were ever at hand in the close fight, promptly administering to the wounded and suffering soldier." Nothing was stated about De Leon leading a charge during either battle. Almost one year later, on August 23, 1847, another commendation was attached referring to, among others, Dr. De Leon: "The medical corps, consisting of Surgeons Satterlee (Senior) Wright, Assistant Surgeons Simpson, DeLeon, Simons, Holder, Roberts, and Deyerle, present claims to especial thanks and admiration-ever among the most fearless, and indifferent to hazard during the conflict." Once again, nothing is stated about him leading any charges.

The Treaty of Guadalupe Hidalgo ended the war between the United States and Mexico on February 2, 1848. U.S. territory swelled by 500,000 square miles. The land representing the states of California, Nevada and Utah, as well as most of Arizona and New Mexico and parts of Colorado and Wyoming, was acquired. In turn, the United States paid Mexico $15 million and took over $3 million in debt owed to citizens by Mexico. Finally, as part of the treaty, Mexico accepted the Rio Grande as its border with Texas. Two months later, on April 4, 1848, a letter arrived from Western Division Headquarters, New Orleans. It contained Special Order No. 45, directing Assistant Surgeon De Leon by order of Major General Butler to "accompany Captain Walker 6th Infantry (a wounded officer) from the city of Mexico to this place." Once they arrived in New Orleans, De Leon would then accompany Captain Walker to Albany, New York. After the captain was under the care of family and friends,

De Leon was then ordered to report to Washington, D.C., to the Surgeon General's Office.

Dr. De Leon was stationed at various installations ranging from Fort Moultrie to the Army Medical Board, located in New York, and, by 1852, as far north as Fort Preble, located in South Portland, Maine. This same year, on January 9, 1852, he asked for sixty days' leave for "private business." He asked again on March 10, 1853, for ten days. De Leon was not happy with his placements. De Leon was eventually sent to Carlisle Barracks in Pennsylvania. When he was told that troops were heading to the Southwest, De Leon agreed to accompany them out to Santa Fe. Once again, he found himself stationed in Santa Fe, New Mexico, in August 1854. During his time there, De Leon probably spent a considerable amount of time dealing with mundane tasks such as illnesses, broken bones and injuries from squabbles between soldiers. One such example was a fight between Francis X. Aubrey and Major Richard Hanson Weightman. On August 18, 1854, Aubrey pulled a gun on the army officer and was able to fire only into the ceiling. When the two men physically scuffled, Major Weightman was able to pull a Bowie knife from his belt. He stabbed Aubrey just above the navel. Whether Dr. De Leon was already there or he was called, according to Ralph Emerson Twitchell in his book *Leading Facts of New Mexican History*, De Leon dressed the wound. However, the knife wound was a fatal one, and Aubrey died about "ten minutes after he was cut."

A great source for re-creating De Leon's life is other people's writings—in one case an army clerk in Santa Fe named Charles E. Whilden, whose letters from 1855 to 1856 survive. In a particular letter dated from Santa Fe, New Mexico, September 27, 1855, he wrote, "Among the Officers stationed here is Dr De Leon from Columbia S.C. He is a nephew of old Dr [Abraham] De Leon of Camden, & a very fine man—I told him that I had a nephew named De Leon &c, and on the strength of it he gave me a dinner at the Officers quarters—We had a good time." The army clerk was a native of South Carolina and would go on to serve in the Confederate army. Roughly two months later, according to military returns, Dr. De Leon "joined by transfer from Santa Fe November 19, 1855."

In February 1856, the military returns for his post indicated that he was absent with leave for seven days starting on February 23. It does not state why he was absent. According to the same military returns, he was back on post by March 7, 1856, and present for duty until August 31, 1856. On that day, he was sent to Los Lunas. Dr. De Leon still found time to socialize while out west.

After Santa Fe, Dr. De Leon made his way to Albuquerque, New Mexico. It is through other soldiers' writings that we are given a glimpse of what Dr. De Leon's routine looked like. One individual was James A. Bennett, who kept a diary from 1850 to 1856. According to an entry in his diary recorded on June 26, 1856, Bennett was sent to the hospital to recover under the care of De Leon. Bennett wrote that he had been wounded during a skirmish with Native Americans. In the summer of 1856, Dr. David Camden de Leon continued climbing up the ranks in the army. He was promoted to surgeon with the rank of major.

Dr. Dauber, in his journal article, wrote that he De Leon requested a transfer to Washington, D.C. He requested a leave of absence so he could see his family, whom he had not seen in some time. It is unclear if he was suffering from ill health or just wanted a break from army life or to visit his brother in Europe. Just prior to the appointment to Washington, D.C., De Leon asked for a leave of absence. The official paperwork housed in the National Archives disclosed that he felt his "state of health might be improved by a visit to Europe." His leave of absence was approved by Special Order 243 in 1859. It is important to note that he was not asking for sick leave. We know from letters written by his brother Edwin and David that he communicated with and visited his brother Edwin, who was the U.S. consul to Egypt. David traveled extensively, including Jerusalem, Constantinople, the Middle East and even North Africa. In a letter to his brother, he wrote that he did not feel these places helped to restore his health. Once in Europe, he felt that his health was really starting to be restored. In the letter, he noted that "all the time I was in the East, I suffered from an unaccountable mental depression foreign to my naturally sanguine temperament....As soon as I sniffed the pure air of the Danube, all my physical and mental elasticity returned, and I could eat and sleep with the grayest." Some have argued that the sectional issues in the United States might have been affecting him when he wrote this letter in August 1860. His leave had already expired when he wrote the letter to Edwin, having expired on June 14, 1860.

After Abraham Lincoln was elected president of the United States, South Carolina was the first state to leave the Union on December 20, 1860. Perhaps it was the events back home that were affecting him? We will never know. However, events would move rapidly after South Carolina left the Union. The Confederate States of America was formed as a separate country from the United States. This occurred on February 8, 1861. Roughly one month later, Abraham Lincoln was sworn in as the nation's sixteenth president. By this time, Dr. De Leon was already back in the South. He penned a letter to his brother Edwin, who he sometimes called Ned, almost a year after his leave had expired.

On June 28, 1861, he wrote a letter to Edwin from Fayetteville in North Carolina, which had left the Union in May 1861. In this letter, he is clearly torn by his commitment as a soldier loyal to his country and to the South. In perhaps one of his most quoted passages in this letter, he wrote that "treason and patriotism are next door neighbors and in accident makes you strike the right knocker. Revolution is treason even if right, if unsuccessful." He continued in another part of the letter: "I have loved my country, I have fought under its flag, and every star and stripe is dear to me." This being acknowledged, he continued as if debating with himself: "A Southern Confederacy acknowledged or inaugurated, then I shall take my stand....If I join a Southern Confederacy I will love the Confederacy as I have my country, not as a section but the whole." It might be strange for people living in the United States today to understand that many people had more loyalty to their state than their country as a whole. This is summed up in a letter written by Robert E. Lee in February 1861: "My loyalty to Virginia ought to take precedence over that which is due to the federal government. If Virginia stands by the old Union, so will I. But, if she secedes, then I will still follow my native state with my sword, and need be with my life." Dr. David Camden de Leon was faced with the same decision. It was finally made in a letter of resignation on February 19, 1861, a little over a week after the Confederate States of America was formed. It was short and to the point: "I have the honor to tender to the President of the United States my resignation of the appointment of Surgeon in the Army of the United States to take effect immediately." What happened next is probably part true and part not.

Many officers resigned their commissions when their respective states left the Union. There is no doubt that Winfield Scott, the commanding general of the U.S. Army, did know De Leon from his time serving during the Mexican-American War. De Leon had been with the general when he was at the head of the army that conquered Mexico City in 1847. In fact, Scott had served in the military for more than fifty years and, in 1861, was the commander in chief of the U.S. Army. Almost ten years later, in his obituary, a confrontation began to appear between Scott and De Leon. In this obituary, it is stated that after handing in his resignation directly to Scott, Scott tried to convince De Leon to stay in the U.S. Army. Pleading with one of the most senior doctors in the army, he was willing to station him away from the action, where he would not be faced with fighting his beloved South. When De Leon seemed to demur, "Old Fuss and Feathers," as Scott was still called, threatened him with arrest. The story goes that De Leon had to secretly leave Washington, D.C. This is probably folklore surrounding De Leon's resignation. What we do know comes by way of the diary of Mary Chesnut. She wrote that De Leon told her, "General Scott does all he can to keep officers from resigning, promising never to send them South." As at least one historian stated to me, threatening De Leon with arrest was out of character for Scott. More than likely, he probably did try to convince De Leon and gave him some time to think about it. After he resigned, she again wrote in her diary that "DeLeon wanted to be Surgeon General." This was entered into her diary between February 27 and March 1, 1861.

President Davis called on De Leon to organize the medical department. He was appointed acting surgeon general of the Confederate army because he was the most senior officer in the U.S. Army before his resignation. More senior officers might not have wanted the job or had not resigned from the U.S. Army yet. This would change in the future. However, prior to his appointment, as acting surgeon general, he was appointed as a medical director and purveyor of medical supplies. A purveyor would oversee acquiring medical supplies for the army, which were desperately needed. De Leon was working for General Braxton Bragg, who was headquartered in Pensacola, Florida, with the Army of Pensacola, according to De Leon's Civil War record, located in the National Archives. His appointment was effective on March 31, when military returns showed De Leon as the chief of medical staff to General Braxton Bragg. Then on April 1, 1861, De Leon was assigned as chief of the medical department for the Army of Pensacola, and then he was later transferred to New Orleans on April 6, 1861. De Leon was directed "in regard to the medical stores formerly belonging to the United States in New Orleans" to secure them and eventually distribute them to those in need. He was directed to communicate with the governor of Louisiana, Thomas Moore. Samuel Cooper, the adjutant general and inspector general for the Confederate army, told De Leon that a large portion of the medical supplies was believed to be located at Fort Pike.

On April 9, 1861, he was in New Orleans writing to the secretary of war for the Confederacy, LeRoy Pope Walker, in Montgomery, Alabama. The Confederate capital had not yet been moved to Richmond. Dr. De Leon wrote, "I have the honor to report that the Governor of Louisiana has turned over to me the public property of the medical department captured from the United States....I will send off to-morrow supplies sufficient for Pensacola." By April 22, 1861, De Leon was assigned to duty as medical director and purveyor at New Orleans and reported to the commander of the Military District of Louisiana, David Emmanuel Twiggs. De Leon continued in this position until May 6, 1861. He was relieved as medical director and purveyor at New Orleans by Acting Assistant Surgeon J.M. Harden, who ordered him to Montgomery, Alabama. De Leon was to assume the duties of acting surgeon general of the Confederacy.

By May 6, 1861, he was told that it would become his job to organize the Medical Department of the Confederacy. His appointment would not last long. His brother Thomas Cooper De Leon wrote in his book, *Four Years in Rebel Capitals*, that while De Leon served as acting surgeon general, "the Medical Department—to play so important and needful a part in the coming days of blood—was now thoroughly reorganized and placed on really efficient footing." Dr. De Leon was replaced by Charles H. Smith on July 12, 1861. According to Guy A Hasegawa in *Matchless Organization: The Confederate Army Medical Department*, his reassignment might have been due to a complaint that he was not adequately supplying the Army of Northern Virginia. This complaint was voiced in the *Charleston Mercury* newspaper on July 30, 1861, in an article titled "The Whereabouts of Beauregard." The journalist wrote that after the Battle of Bull Run, or Manassas, the "incapacity, neglect, or want of organization of the Surgeon Generals and Commissariat Departments is vehemently condemned." The journalist, who is not listed, continued to believe that because of a lack of supplies, surgeons could not alleviate the suffering of troops after and during the battle. Charles H. Smith retained the position for a short period of time but was replaced by Samuel Preston Moore, who became the first surgeon general of the Confederacy and would retain that office until the end of the Civil War. Moore replaced Smith on July 30, 1861, by Special Order No. 110 from the new capital of Richmond, "where Surgeon Samuel P. Moore, Medical Department, is assigned to duty in this city as acting Surgeon-General, C.S. Army. He will relieve Surg. Charles H. Smith, in charge of the Medical Bureau by command of the Secretary of War."

David's brother, Thomas, defended his accomplishments when he wrote that David was on the board to "pass the preliminary design for a service uniform." He also organized the medical department. According to Frank R. Freeman in his book *Gangrene and Glory: Medical Care During the American Civil War*, if this were not enough, with a yearly budget of $365,000,

David acquired several of Richmond's largest buildings to use as hospitals. Unfortunately, these hospitals were not adequate. They were quickly overrun after the Battle of Bull Run—perhaps adding to the dissatisfaction articulated in the newspaper stated in the *Charleston Mercury.*

Once he was dismissed as acting surgeon general, De Leon was transferred to Norfolk, Virginia, where again his organizational skills were put to good use when he became the medical director and purveyor for General Benjamin Huger. After being stationed in Norfolk, according to his orders on June 3, 1862, he was made medical director of the Army of Northern Virginia under General Robert E. Lee. This was part of General Order No. 60. Dr. David Camden de Leon's time with Lee lasted about a month.

The Encyclopedia of Virginia describes the Seven Days' Battle, which was fought from June 25 to July 1, 1862, as "the decisive engagements of the Peninsula Campaign during the American Civil War." Hasegawa wrote that De Leon was thrown from his horse in June 1862 while on the battlefield. According to his military record, he was relieved on June 27, 1862. Whatever his injury, it forced him to resign his commission with the Army of Northern Virginia later in the summer of 1862. According to his record, his resignation was accepted on August 1, 1862. His letter does not state the nature of his injuries. In an article written by Perry M. DeLeon for *American Jewish Historical Quarterly*, it was argued that after David Camden de Leon recovered, he became the medical director of John Bankhead Magruder, who was the ranking officer in the District of Texas, New Mexico and Arizona. His forces were known for being able to temporarily lift the Union blockade of Galveston, Texas, in 1863.

America's Civil War came to an end in the spring of 1865. It did not end for all of the Confederacy. Many former Confederates, including De Leon, left the United States and moved to Mexico. Eventually, De Leon came back and settled in New Mexico Territory in 1866, where he would spend the remainder of his life as a doctor in Santa Fe. It is believed that he never returned to South Carolina and did not communicate on a regular basis with his family. Why he did this is open to conjecture. He was living in Santa Fe in the last federal census and was listed as a "Doctor of Medicine." It is believed that he owned property in New Mexico. His age was listed as fifty-two years.

A letter to Edwin from his sister, dated September 20, 1872, announced the death of his brother: "Yesterday at dinner a letter was handed me with the sad and sudden announcement of the death if our dear brother in

New Mexico. It occurred on 3d September—no particulars of his illness or anything." This letter continued, "To die all alone in that far away god [*sic*] forsaken country is a sad end indeed." He was just fifty-four years old and had never married. According to an obituary, he died in Sister's Hospital. According to the *Richmond Dispatch*, his last years were "darkened by exile, disease, and suffering." Where he was buried is no longer known.

Bibliography

General Resources

Adams, George Worthington. *Doctors in Blue: The Medical History of the Union Army in the Civil War*. Louisiana State University Press, 1950.

Blanton, DeAnne, and Lauren M. Cook. *They Fought Like Demons: Women Soldiers in the Civil War*. Louisiana State University Press, 2002.

Boatner, Mark B., III. *Civil War Dictionary*. David McKay Company Inc., 1987.

Cozzens, Peter, ed. *Battles & Leaders of the Civil War*. Vol. 5. University of Illinois Press, 2002.

Dougherty, Kevin J., and John D. Wright. *The Civil War: A Military History*. Amber Books, 2022.

Eggleston, Larry G. *Women in the Civil War: Extraordinary Stories of Soldiers, Spies, Nurses, Doctors, Crusaders, and Others*. McFarland and Company, 2003.

Guelzo, Allen C. *Gettysburg: The Last Invasion*. Vintage Books, 2013.

Journal of the Congress of the Confederate States of America, 1861–1865. 7 vols. 58th Congress, 2nd Session, 1904–05, [S. Doc 234].

McPherson, James M. *Battle Cry of Freedom*. Oxford University Press, 1988.

———. *Crossroads of Freedom: Antietam*. Oxford University Press, 2002.

———. *For Causes and Comrades: Why Men Fought in the Civil War*. Oxford University Press, 1997.

National Park Service. *Hispanics and the Civil War: From the Battlefield to Homefront*. Government Printing Office, 2011.

Pryor, Elizabeth Brown. *Clara Barton: Professional Angel*. University of Pennsylvania Press, 1987.

U.S. War Department. *War of the Rebellion: A Compilation of the Official Records of the Union and Confederate Armies*. 128 vols. Government Printing Office, 1880–1900.

AUGUSTO RODRIGUEZ

Approved Pension File for Sergeant Augustus Rodriqucz, Company I, 15th Connecticut Infantry Regiment. Record Group 15, Records of the Department of Veterans Affairs, 1773–2007. National Archives and Records Administration, Washington, D.C.

Compiled Service Record, Civil War, 2nd Lieutenant Augustus Rodriques, Company I, 15th Connecticut. Infantry Regiment. Record Group 94. National Archives and Records Administration, Washington, D.C.

Connecticut Adjutant-General's Office. *Catalogue of Connecticut Volunteer Organizations (Infantry, Cavalry, and Artillery) in the Service of the United States, 1861–1865: with Additional Enlistments, Casualties, &c., &c., and Brief Summaries Showing the Operations and Service of the Several Regiments and Batteries*. Brown & Gross, 1869.

Connecticut State Library. *Probate Files Collection, Early to 1880*. Hartford, Connecticut.

Dyer, Frederick. *Compendium of the War of the Rebellion*. Dyer Publishing Company, 1908.

Gustave Rodriguez Death Certificate, March 22, 1880. State of Connecticut. Copy in possession of author.

Hewett, Janet. *Supplement to the Official Records of the Union and Confederate Armies*. Part II, *Record of Events*. Broadfoot Publishing Company, 1994.

Hewett, Janet B., et al. *Supplement to the Official Records of the Union and Confederate Armies*. 51 vols. Compiled Military Service Record of 2nd Lieutenant Augustus Rodriques, Company I, 15th Connecticut Infantry Regiment. Broadfoot Publishing Company, 1994–97.

National Archives and Records Administration. Consolidated Lists of Civil War Draft Registration Records (Provost Marshal General's Bureau; Consolidated Enrollment Lists, 1863–1865). Record Group: 110; Collection Name: Consolidated Enrollment Lists, 1863–65 (Civil War Union Draft Records); NAI: 4213514; Archive vol. no. 4 of 4.

Record of Service of Connecticut Men, Army, and Navy, in the War of the Rebellion. Case, Lockwood & Brainard Company, 1889.

Sheldon Thorpe Diary, 1856–1923. North Haven Historical Society.

Thorpe, Sheldon B. *The History of the Fifteenth Connecticut Volunteers in the War for the Defense of the Union, 1861–1865.* Price, Lee & Adkins Company, 1893.

U.S. Bureau of the Census. "U.S. Census of Population." Government Printing Office, 1860, 1870, 1880.

War Department Library. *Reunions of Ct. Regiments for 1896.* Washington, D.C.

Philip Bazaar

Bazan, Philip. Massachusetts Treasury correspondence. Commonwealth of Massachusetts State Archives.

Commonwealth of Massachusetts State Archives. Records of the Commonwealth of Massachusetts, Paymaster General Enlistment Bounty.

———. Records of the Commonwealth of Massachusetts, Roster of Massachusetts Naval Enlistments.

Congressional Medal of Honor Society. "Stories of Sacrifice." https://www.cmohs.org/recipients/philip-bazaar.

Find a Grave. "Philip Bazaar." https://www.findagrave.com/memorial/93477687/philip-bazaar.

Higginson, Thomas Wentworth. *Massachusetts in the Army and Navy During the War of 1861–1865.* Vols. 1 and 2. Wright and Porter, 1895.

Irma and Paul Milstein Division of United States History, Local History and Genealogy. "New York City Directory." New York Public Library Digital Collections. https://digitalcollections.nypl.org/258b7470-5361-0134-8a14-0050568a51c.

Kernan, Joe. "The Honor Was Just the Beginning." *Cranston Herald*, November 2, 2012. https://cranstononline.com/stories/the-honor-was-just-the-beginning,76438.

Massachusetts Adjutant-General's Office. *Annual Report of the Adjutant-General of the Commonwealth of Massachusetts.* Boston Wright and Potter, 1865.

Naval History and Heritage Command. "Santiago de Cuba (Side Wheel Steamer)." https://www.history.navy.mil/content/history/archive/research-archive/histories/ship-histories/danfs/danfs-archvies/santiago-de-cuba.html.

Navy Department, Bureau of Navigation, to Major Edward T. Bouve, Washington, D.C., March 11, 1916.

North Carolina Historic Sites. "The Forces First Expedition Against Fort Fisher December 24–27, 1864." https://historicsites.nc.gov/all-sites/fort-fisher/history/civil-war-ft-fisher/forces.

———. "Such a Hell of Noise." https://historic sites.nc.gov/allsites/fort-fisher/history/civil-war-ft-fisher/2nd-attack.

U.S. Bureau of the Census. "U.S. Census of Population." Government Printing Office, 1900, 1910.

U.S. Navy. *General Records of the Department of the Navy, 1798–1947*. Record Group 80, National Archives and Records Administration.

Welles, Gideon. *Report of the Secretary of the Navy, with an Appendix Containing Reports from Officers*. Government Printing Office, 1865.

David Glasgow Farragut

Adelson, Bruce. *David Farragut: Union Admiral*. Infobase Publishing, 2001.

Barnes, James. *David G. Farragut*. Small, Maynard & Company, 1899.

———. *Midshipman Farragut*. D. Appleton and Company, 1909.

Certificate of Appointment for Loyall Farragut as a Cadet Effective September 1, 1863, Signed Edwin Stanton, Secretary of War, February 22, 1864. IV, Box: 1, Folder: 16. David G. Farragut Papers, MS-1887. Betsey B. Creekmore Special Collections and University Archives, University of Tennessee, Knoxville.

Duffy, James P. *Lincoln's Admiral: The Civil War Campaigns of David Farragut*. New Word City Inc., 1997.

Farragut, Loyall. *The Life of David Glasgow Farragut, First Admiral of the United States Navy: Embodying His Journal and Letters*. D. Appleton and Company, 1879.

General Order No. 9, dated Flag Ship Hartford, off Mobile Bay, July 6, 1864. I, Box: 1, Folder: 6. David G. Farragut Papers, MS-1887. Betsey B. Creekmore Special Collections and University Archives, University of Tennessee, Knoxville.

Gideon Welles to Virginia Farragut, dated Hartford, September 5, 1870. III, Box: 1, Folder: 15. David G. Farragut Papers, MS-1887. Betsey B. Creekmore Special Collections and University Archives, University of Tennessee, Knoxville.

Hattendorf, John B., and D.G. Farragut. "A Long-Lost Farragut Letter Is Rediscovered." *Naval War College Review* 24, no. 4 (1971): 97–100. http://www.jstor.org/stable/44639665.

Hickman, Kennedy. "Admiral David G. Farragut: Hero of the Union Navy." *New York Times*, September 27, 2011.

Loyall Farragut to David Farragut, dated Hastings on the Hudson, May 5, 1862. I, Box: 1, Folder: 3. David G. Farragut Papers, MS-1887. Betsey B. Creekmore Special Collections and University Archives, University of Tennessee, Knoxville.

Loyall Farragut to David Farragut, dated West Point, September 1, 1864. I, Box: 1, Folder: 6. David G. Farragut Papers, MS-1887. Betsey B. Creekmore Special Collections and University Archives, University of Tennessee, Knoxville.

Machado, Lieutenant Commander Rolando. "'Damn the Torpedoes—Full Speed Ahead': Navy's First Admiral Was Hispanic Hero." U.S. Navy, September 15, 2020. https://www.navy.mil/Press-Office/News-Stories/Article/2347790/damn-the-torpedoes-full-speed-ahead-navys-first-admiral-was-hispanic-hero.

Mahan, Alfred Thayer. *Admiral Farragut*. D. Appleton and Company, 1892.

Martin, Christopher. *Damn the Torpedoes!: The Story of America's First Admiral: David Glasgow Farragut*. Abelard-Schuman, 1970.

Naval History and Heritage Command. "David Glasgow Farragut 5 July 1801–14 August 1870." https://www.history.navy.mil/research/library/research-guides/z-files/zb-files/zb-files-f/farragut-davidg.html.

Shorto, Russell. *David Farragut and the Great Naval Blockade*. Silver Burdett Press, 1991.

Soley, James Russell. *Admiral Porter*. D. Appleton, 1903.

Stein, R. Conrad. *David Farragut: First Admiral of the U.S. Navy*. Chelsea House Publishers, 2005.

Tenney, W.J. *The Military and Naval History of the Rebellion in the United States*. D. Appleton, 1867.

FEDERICO AND ADOLFO CAVADA

Abraham Lincoln Papers, Series 1, General Correspondence, 1833–1916. Green Clay Smith to Abraham Lincoln [with Endorsement by Lincoln] March 16, 1864. Manuscript/Mixed Material, Library of Congress. http://www.loc.gov/resource/ma/3162100.

———. Robert E. Petersen to Abraham Lincoln, October 3, 1864. Manuscript/Mixed Material, Library of Congress. https://www.loc.gov/resource/mal3693800.

American Battlefield Trust. "Adolfo Fernandez Cavada." https://www.battlefield.org/learn/biographies/adolfo-fernandez-cavada.

———. "Chancellorsville." https://www.battlefield.org/learn/civil-war/battles/chancellorsville.

———. "Fredericksburg." https://www.battlefield.org/learn/civil-war/battles/fredericksburg.

Associated Alumni of Central High School. *The Handbook of the Central High School of Philadelphia*, 1951–55. 13th ed. Mary Gaston Barnwell Foundation, 1955.

Bates, Samuel B. *History of Pennsylvania Volunteers, 1861–85*. 5 vols. B. Singerly State Printers, 1871.

Cavada, Adolfo Fernandez. "Adolfo Fernandez Cavada Diary, 1861–1863." Transcribed by Professor Antonio Rafael de la Cova. Historical Society of Pennsylvania.

Cavada, F.F. *Libby Life: Experiences of a Prisoner of War in Richmond, VA, 1863–1864*. Philadelphia King and Baird, 1864.

Collis, Charles H.T. *Case of F.F. Cavada*. King and Baird, 1865.

Davis, Oliver Wilson. *Sketch of Frederic Fernandez Cavada: A Native of Cuba*. James B. Chandler, 1871.

Encyclopedia Virginia. "Chancellorsville Campaign." https://encyclopediavirginia.org/entries/chancellorville-campaign.

Fessenden, Oran Otis. "Panama Railroad." *Harper's New Monthly Magazine* 20 (December 1859–May 1860).

Fredericksburg and Spotsylvania National Military Park, National Park Service. "The Battle of Chancellorsville." http://www.nps.gov/frsp/learn/historyculture/chist.htm.

Gettysburg National Military Park. "The Cavada Brothers: Two Soldiers, Two Wars." https://npsgnmp.wordpress.com/2012/05/10/the-cavada-brothers-two-soldiers-two-wars.

Hagerty, Edward J. *Collis' Zouaves*. Louisiana State University Press, 2005.

Humphrey, Henry H. *Andrew Atkinson Humphrey: A Biography*. John C. Winston Company, 1924.

Latin American Studies. "Memoirs of Alexander Wallace Givin, 114th Pennsylvania Volunteers Infantry Regiment." https://www/latinamericanstudies.org/cavada/givin-memoirs.htm.

National Park Service. "The Civil War Union: Pennsylvania Infantry 114th Regiment, Pennsylvania Infantry." Ahttps://www.nps/civilwar/search-battle-units-details.htm?battleunitecode=UPA0114RI.

Pennsylvania Civil War Muster Rolls and Related Records, 1861–1866. Records of the Department of Military and Veterans Affairs, Records Group 19, Series 1911. Pennsylvania Historical and Museum Commission, Harrisburg, Pennsylvania.

Percy, Matthew T. "Nothing but the Spirit of Heroism: Andrew A. Humphreys at Chancellorsville and Gettysburg." *Army History*, no. 88 (Summer 2013): 6–37.

Samuel Dutton Letter. Papers Relating to Citizens, Compiled 1861–1865. Record Group 109, National Archives and Records Administration, Washington, D.C.

Tribune (Scranton, Pennsylvania). "General Cavada." July 11, 1871.

U.S. Letters Received by the Office of the Adjutant General, 1861–1870. Roll 0261. "A.A. Humphreys." National Archives and Records Administration, Washington, D.C.

U.S. Union Citizens File, 1861–1865. Samuel Dutton Maryland, 1864. M345 National Archives and Records Administration.

University of Miami Digital Collections, Federico Fernandez-Cavada Collection. https://digitalcollectionslibraryMiami.edu/digital/collection/chc5006.

The War of the Rebellion: A Compilation of the Official Records of the Union and Confederate Armies. "Lieutenant Colonel Robert N. Scott." Series I, Vol. 25, in two parts. Part I—Reports. Government Printing Office, 1889.

Maria Dolores "Lola" Sánchez

American Battlefield Trust. "Lola Sachez: Confederate Spy." https://www. battlefields.org/learn/biographies/lola-sachez.

Caban, Pedro, Barbara Cruz and Jose Carrasco. *The Latino Experience in United States History*. Globe Pearson, 1994.

Census Department of the South, November 1864, for Jacksonville, Fernandina and St. Augustine. Florida Department of the South, Hilton Head, South Carolina.

Chisolm, William D. "True Heroine for the Confederacy to Be Honored." *Columbia (SC) Star*, 2008.

Confederate Veteran 17 (August 1909).

Connecticut Adjutant-General's Office. *The First Regiment, Connecticut Volunteer Heavy Artillery in the War of the Rebellion, 1861–1865*. Lockwood & Brainard, 1889.

Cuevas, Rebecca M. "Hispanic Confederate Heritage—The Sánchez Sister." Bella Online. https://www.bellaonline.com/articles/art40197.asp.

Downtown Palatka Inc. "Gem City of the St. Johns River." http://www. palatkadowntown.com/palatka-history.html.

Eggleston, Larry G. *Women in the Civil War: Extraordinary Stories of Soldiers, Spies, Nurses, Doctors, Crusaders, and Others*. McFarland and Company, 2003.

Fairbanks, George R. *Florida: Its History and Its Romance*. 2nd ed. H. and W.B. Drew Company, 1901.

Find a Grave. "Maria Dolores Lopez." https://www.findagrave.com/ memorial/253425401/maria-dolores-lopez.

Frank, Lisa. *Women in the American Civil War*. Vol. 1. ABC-Clio, 2008.

Gladwin, William J., Jr. *Men, Salt, Cattle and Battle: The Civil War in Florida, November 1860–July 1865*. Naval War College, 1992.

Hahn, Laurie. "Full Steam Ahead: Steam Boating on the St. Johns River." *Daytona Beach News-Journal*, December 15, 2021. http://www. newsjournalonline.com/story/news/2021/12/15/fullsteam-ahead-steamboating-st-johns-river-Florida/6494719001.

Jones, Allen W. "Military Events in Florida During the Civil War, 1861– 1865." *Florida Historical Quarterly* 39, no. 1 (1960): 42–45. https://stars. library.ucf.edu/fhq/vol39/iss1/6.

Liles, Deborah M., and Angela Boswell, eds. *Women in Civil War Texas*. University of North Texas Press, 2016.

Mack, William B., and Irvin D.S. Winsboro. "Blue Water, Brown Water, and Confederate Disloyalty: The Peculiar and Personal Naval Conflict in South Florida during the Civil War." *Florida Historical Quarterly* 9, no. 1 (Summer 2011): 34–60.

Miller, Joseph E. "General J.J. Dickison (1816–1902)." *Jacksonville Observer*, April 14, 2010.

Redd, Robert. *St. Augustine and the Civil War*. The History Press, 2014.

Schafer, Daniel L. *Thunder on the River: The Civil War in Northwest Florida*. University of Florida Press, 2010.

Strickland, Alice. "Blockage Runner." *Florida Historical Quarterly* 36, no.2 (1957): 85–93. https://stars.library.ucf.edu/fhq/vol36/iss2/3.

Underwood, J.L. *The Women of the Confederacy*. Neale Publishing, 1906.

Wynne, Nick, and Joe Crankshaw. *Florida Civil War Blockades: Battling for the Coast History*. The History Press, 2011.

Thomas Hernandez

Buker, George E. *Blockades, Refugees, & Contraband*. University of Alabama Press, 1993.

Dickson, James, Jr. *Diary of James Dickson, Jr. December 16–22, 1861*. University of Georgia Libraries Manuscript Collection 791.

Digital Library of Georgia. "Directories for Savannah, Georgia," https://dig.usg.edu/collection/gsc_savcd.

Ford, Samuel Blatch. *Reports of Cases in Prize, 1861–1865*. Government Printing Office, 1866.

Moore, Frank. *The Rebellion Record: A Diary of American Events Edited by Frank Moore*. Vol. 3. G.P. Putnam, 1862.

Orvin, Clayton Maxwell. *In South Carolina Waters, 1861–1865*. Nelsons Southern Printing and Publishing Company, 1961.

Quarstein, John V. "Battle of Wassaw Sound and CSS Atlanta." Mariners' Museum and Park. https://www.marinersmuseum.org/2021/07/battle-of-wassaw-sound-and-css-atlanta.

Thomas Hernandez, Indigent Pension Application No. 2060, 1897. Confederate Pension Applications. Georgia Confederate Pension Office, RG 59-1-1, Georgia Archives.

U.S. Bureau of the Census. U.S. Census of Population. Government Printing Office, 1880, 1900, 1870, 1860, 1850.

Wise, Stephen R. *Lifeline of the Confederacy: Blockade Running During the Civil War*. University of South Carolina Press, 1991.

LORETA JANETA VELÁZQUEZ

Blanton, DeAnne, and Lauren M. Cook. *They Fought Like Demons: Women Soldiers in the Civil War*. Louisiana State University Press, 2002.

Chattanooga Daily Rebel. "Lieutenant Buford." August 4, 1863. Newspaper Archive.

Cincinnati Enquirer. "A Female Lieutenant Mrs. Mary De Caulp." January 23, 1867. Newspaper Archive.

Civil War Richmond. www.civilwarrichmond.com.

Coski, John. "Loreta Velasquez Letters." www.ACWM.org/blog/July-2016-documents-month-loreta-velasqucz-letters.

Daily Gazette. "The Woman in Battle." May 5, 1877. Newspaper Archive.

Davis, William C. *Inventing Loreta Velasquez: Confederate Soldier Impersonator, Media Celebrity, and Con Artist*. Southern Illinois University Press, 2016.

Hoffert, Sylvia D. "Heroine or Hoaxer." *Civil War Illustrated* (June 1978).

New Orleans Daily Picayune. January 5, 1867.

Richmond Daily Examiner. September 15, 1863.

Staunton Spectator. "Sent South." July 21, 1863.

Velázquez, Loreta Janeta. *The Woman in Battle: A Narrative of the Exploits, Adventures and Travels of Madame Loreta Janeta Velázquez, Otherwise Known as Lieutenant Harry T. Buford, Confederate States Army*. Dustin, Gilman & Company, 1876.

DAVID CAMDEN DE LEON

Bennett, J.A. *A Dragoon in New Mexico*. University of New Mexico Press, 1948.

Burns, Stanley B. "David Camden DeLeon." *Judeo Medical Journal* 2 (December 2001–January 2002): 8.

Charleston Daily Courier. "David C. DeLeon." September 24, 1872. Newspaper Archive.

Charleston Daily News. "Death of a South Carolinian Abroad: David Camden DeLeon." September 25, 1872. Newspaper Archive.

Chesnut, Mary Boykin. *Mary Chesnut's Civil War*. Edited by C. Vann Woodward. Yale University Press, 1981.

———. *The Private Mary Chesnut: The Unpublished Civil War Diaries*. Edited by C. Vann Woodward and Elisabeth Muhlenfeld. Oxford University Press Publication, 1984.

Compiled Military Service Record, Civil War. Dr. David Camden de Leon. Record Group 109. National Archives and Records Administration, Washington, D.C.

Cullop, Charles P. *Confederate Propaganda in Europe, 1861–1865*. University of Miami Press, 1969.

Cunningham, H.H. *Doctors in Gray: The Confederate Medical Service*. Louisiana State University Press, 1958.

Dauber, Leonard G. "David Camden De Leon, MD Patriot or Traitor." *NYS Journal of Medicine* 70, no. 23 (December 1970).

DeLeon, Cooper Thomas. *Belles, Beaux, and Brass of the '60s*. N.p., 1909.

De Leon, Edwin. *Thirty Years of My Life on Three Continents*. Ward and Downey, 1890.

DeLeon, Perry. "Military Record of the De Leon Family and of Captain Perry M. De Leon." *Publication of the American Jewish Historical Society* 50 no. 4 (June 1961): 332–34.

Edwin DeLeon Papers. MF-486a to MF-486f. Jacob Rader Marcus Center of the American Jewish Archives Cincinnati, Ohio.

Elzas, Barrett A. *The Jews of South Carolina*. J.B. Lippincott Company, 1908.

Freemon, Frank R. *Gangrene and Glory: Medical Care During the American Civil War*. University Illinois Press, 2001.

Hasegawa, Guy R. *Matchless Organization: The Confederate Army Medical Department*. Southern Illinois University Press, 2021.

Message from the President of the United States to the Two House of Congress. *U.S. Congressional Serial Set* (1846): 1–704.

Simonhoff, Harry. "David Camden DeLeon: The Jew of 1846." *Wisconsin Jewish Chronicle*, April 11, 1954. Newspaper Archive.

State of the Union Address. *U.S. Congressional Set* (1847): 1–249.

Twitchell, Ralph Emerson. *The Leading Fact of New Mexico*. Vol. 2. Horn & Wallace, 1963.

U.S. Bureau of the Census. U.S. Census of Population. Government Printing Office, 1850, 1860, 1870.

Whilden, Charles E., and John Hammond Moore. "Letters from a Santa Fe Army Clerk, 1855–1856." *New Mexico Historical Review* 40, no. 2 (1965): 141–64. https//digitalrepository.unm.edu/nmhr/vol40/iss2/4.

Wiernik, Peter. *History of the Jews in America*. Jewish Press Publishing, 1912.

About the Author

*A*J. Schenkman is an award-winning, New York–based writer. Since starting to write for local papers, Schenkman has branched out into writing for magazines, blogs, academic journals and children's books; in history and other subjects, Schenkman is also the author of several books about local, national and regional history.

Visit us at
www.historypress.com
....